The Battle for Illinois

Jonathan N. Hall

HERITAGE BOOKS
2025

HERITAGE BOOKS
AN IMPRINT OF HERITAGE BOOKS, INC.

Books, CDs, and more—Worldwide

For our listing of thousands of titles see our website
at
www.HeritageBooks.com

Published 2025 by
HERITAGE BOOKS, INC.
Publishing Division
5810 Ruatan Street
Berwyn Heights, MD 20740

Copyright © 2025 Jonathan N. Hall

Heritage Books by the author:
The Battle for Illinois
Reconstructed Forts of the Old Northwest Territory

All rights reserved. No part of this book may be reproduced or transmitted in any form or by any means, electronic or mechanical, including photocopying, recording or by any information storage and retrieval system without written permission from the author, except for the inclusion of brief quotations in a review.

International Standard Book Number
Paperbound: 978-0-7884-5065-5

Table of Contents

Introduction v

Part I
The Prehistoric and Colonial Period

Chapter One	Cahokia 1
Chapter Two	Iroquois Wars 7
Chapter Three	Fox Wars 25
Chapter Four	French and Indian War and Pontiac . 39

Part II
The American Revolution

Chapter Five	George Rogers Clark 55
Chapter Six	St. Louis and Cahokia 73
Chapter Seven	Post-American Revolution 79

Part III
The War of 1812

Chapter Eight	Fort Dearborn 93
Chapter Nine	Fort Madison 105
Chapter Ten	Peoria 113
Chapter Eleven	Prairie Du Chien 129
	and Campbell's Island
Chapter Twelve	Credit Island 139
Chapter Thirteen	Between Wars 147

Part IV
The Black Hawk War

Chapter Fourteen	Prelude to War	163
Chapter Fifteen	Stillman's Run	171
Chapter Sixteen	Kellogg's Grove	183
Chapter Seventeen	Apple River Fort	191
	and Second Battle of Kellogg's Grove	
Chapter Eighteen	Wisconsin Heights	201
Chapter Nineteen	Bad Axe	209
Appendix I	1804 Treaty	219
Appendix II	Abraham Lincoln	225
	and other famous people who served in the Black Hawk War	
Appendix III	Reconstructed Forts in Illinois	229
Bibliography		235

Introduction

I have endeavored to write a military history of Illinois divided into four parts, from the time before the earliest French explorers until the conclusion of the Black Hawk War, which ended the Indian occupation of Illinois. I have used accounts of eyewitnesses or earlier historians to describe the battles whenever possible. While not every little skirmish is mentioned, all the major engagements of each war are included. Out of necessity, some of the battles mentioned were fought outside Illinois' boundaries. They are included since Illinois inhabitants fought in them as they were part of the war in which they were involved.

Part I of the book, Prehistoric and Colonial Period, begins with an account written by John Heckewelder obtained from the Delaware Indians describing their encounter with Cahokia in the distant past. Next, the history of the Iroquois War with the Illinois Confederation is told both before and during early French contact. From exploration in the second half of the seventeenth century to settlement in Illinois in the first half of the eighteenth century, the French steadily gained influence over the Illinois Indians. They persuaded them to aid them in their wars, first against the Fox tribe, then in their wars against the Chickasaws, and finally against the English in the French and Indian War. Finally, with Pontiac's Rebellion and its aftermath, the Illinois Indians are significantly reduced in power, and other Indian tribes enter the state. The legend of Starved Rock as a reason for the elimination of the Illinois Indians is also discussed.

In Part II, *The American Revolution,* the campaign of George Rogers Clark, told by himself, provides the basis for the American acquisition of Illinois from the British, who had obtained it from the French after the French and Indian War. There is one attempt by the British and Indians to regain what was lost in the battle for Cahokia. After the American Revolution, Americans began to push into the Northwest Territory and Illinois. They provoke the Indians to resist, fighting in Ohio against Little Turtle's Miami Confederation, in Indiana against the Shawnee Prophet, and the Kickapoo in Illinois. The Indians found a common cause with the British and attempted to push the Americans back in the War of 1812.

In Part III, *The War of 1812,* the Sauk and Fox, the Potawatomi, the Kickapoo, and others fight battles and skirmishes against the Americans inside and outside Illinois borders. They won most battles, from the famous Fort Dearborn massacre in Chicago to Saukenuk, near present-day Rock Island, to Peoria and Fort Madison, just across the Mississippi River in Iowa. Still, they lost the war and most of their territory in Illinois.

Finally, in Part IV, *The Black Hawk War,* the tragic ordeal of the Sauk and Fox under Black Hawk unfolds. Black Hawk's "British band" fights an unwanted hopeless war to retain some land in Illinois and then attempts to flee Illinois and escape back across the Mississippi. Stillman's Run, Kellogg's Grove, Apple River Fort, Wisconsin River, and Bad Axe are all battles detailed in this last war fought in Illinois. With the conclusion of the Black Hawk War, centuries of Indian control of Illinois is terminated.

I have tried to pack as much information as possible into Illinois's brief, overall military history. Many more detailed written accounts of the different wars and battles are mentioned in other books. However, to my knowledge, no previous histories cover all the military events during this entire period in Illinois. This is the reason for writing this book. It is recommended that the reader refer to the bibliography for a deeper understanding of specific wars or battles.

There are differences in the spellings of various words due to different authors' backgrounds and changes in our language over time. Though the information included may be a little awkward in some places, I have avoided using footnotes to make the reading easier. I hope this book will give each reader a greater understanding of the conflicts that changed the control of Illinois from that of the Indians to the French, to the British, and finally to the Americans.

Part I
The Prehistoric and Colonial Period

Chapter One

Cahokia

Who were the first people to inhabit Illinois? As far back as we can determine, different groups of people have warred against each other for possession of this bountiful land, which abounded in wild game, including herds of deer, buffalo, and numerous fish in its lakes and streams. Archaeologists have unearthed evidence that fierce battles occurred in the past. For example, in one ancient burial mound estimated to be from around 1300 A.D. in which two hundred and sixty-four partial and complete skeletons were examined, archaeologists concluded that forty-three of them died a violent death.

These mound builders established an advanced culture centered in Illinois at Cahokia, the largest city in North America north of Mexico. At its peak, the population of Cahokia exceeded 10,000 people, who occupied almost 4000 acres. An additional 20,000-30,000 inhabitants lived in surrounding communities and on farms. The population of Cahokia has been estimated to have reached over 20,000 by 1150 A.D. A wooden stockade two miles in circumference surrounded the central part of the city.

The people in Cahokia practiced agriculture, manufactured copper axes, and drilled pearls. The Cahokia artisans carved stones and bone ware and created terra cotta figurines. They are famous for the immense mounds of heaped-up soil used for burial and temples, numbering over two hundred at once. The present cluster of mounds in Cahokia is the greatest in the United States, consisting of over eighty mounds. Monks Mound, at about one hundred feet high, with a base larger than the Great Pyramid at Giza, was the third largest in the world.

Though the real reason for the demise of the Cahokians is unknown, considering their fortifications, warfare likely played an important part. Caddoan-speaking groups of Indians such as the Pawnee, Wichita, and Arikara tribes are believed to be the most direct descendent of the Cahokians, with indications that Omaha, Ponca, Dakota, Hidatsa, Mandan, Cheyenne, and possibly Crow tribes also were linked to the Cahokians. This has been determined mainly by the location of Cahokia artifacts found by archaeologists and through cultural similarities of the above tribes to the Cahokians. For example, the game Chunkey, played with a rolling stone, was enjoyed by these same tribes.

One reason for the demise of the Cahokians should be related to John Heckewelder, a pastor to the Moravian Indians for fifty years. In the second half of the eighteenth century, he wrote down the traditions of the Delaware Indians who had converted to Christianity. In his book *History, Manners, and Customs of the Indian Nations: Who Once Inhabited Pennsylvania and the Neighboring States,* he describes their migration from the West. In his retelling of the traditional history of the Delaware (Lenni Lenape), the Delaware and the Iroquois were responsible for bringing about the fall of Cahokia. Heckewelder's account is as follows.

> The Lenni Lenape (according to the traditions handed down to them by their ancestors) resided many hundred years ago in a distant country in the western part of the American continent. For some reason, which I do not find accounted for,

they determined on migrating to the eastward, and accordingly set out together in a body. After a very long journey, and many night's encampments by the way, they at length arrived on the Namaesi Sipu (Mississippi River), where they fell in with the Mengwe (Iroquois), who had likewise emigrated from a distant country, and had struck upon this river somewhat higher up. Their object was the same with that of the Delawares; they were proceeding on to the eastward, until they should find a country that pleased them. The spies which the Lenape had sent forward for the purpose of reconnoitering, had long before their arrival discovered that the country east of the Mississippi was inhabited by a very powerful nation, who had many large towns built on the best rivers flowing through their land. Those people (as I was told) called themselves *Talligeu or Talligewi.* Colonel John Gibson, however, a gentleman who has a thorough knowledge of the Indians, and speaks several of their languages, is of opinion that they were not called *Talligewi,* but *Alligewi,* and it would seem that he is right, from the traces of their name which still remain in the country, the Allegheny river and mountains have indubitably been named after them. The Delawares still call the former *Alligewi Sipu,* the River of the Alligewi. We have adopted, I know not for what reason, its Iroquois name, Ohio, which the French had literally translated into *La Belle Riviere,* The Beautiful River. A branch of it, however, still retains the ancient name Allegheny.

  Many wonderful things are told of this famous people. They are said to have been remarkably tall and stout, and there is a tradition that there were giants among them, people of much larger size than the tallest of the Lenape. It is related that they had built to themselves regular fortifications or entrenchments, from whence they would sally out, but were generally repulsed. .....

When the Lenape arrived on the banks of the Mississippi they sent a message to the Alligewi to request permission to settle themselves in their neighborhood. This was refused them, but they obtained leave to pass through the country and seek a settlement farther to the eastward. They accordingly began to cross the Namaesi Sipu, when the Alligewi, seeing that their numbers were so very great, and in fact they consisted of many thousands, made a furious attack on those who had crossed, threatening them all with destruction if they dared to persist in coming over to their side of the river. Fired at the treachery of these people, and the great loss of men they had sustained, and besides, not being prepared for a conflict, the Lenape consulted on what was to be done; whether to retreat in the best manner they could, or try their strength, and let the enemy see that they were not cowards, but men, and too high-minded to suffer themselves to be driven off before they had made a trial of their strength, and were convinced that the enemy was too powerful for them. The Mengwe, who had hitherto been satisfied with being spectators from a distance, offered to join them, on condition that, after conquering the country, they should be entitled to share it with them; their proposal was accepted, and the resolution was taken by the two nations, to conquer or die.

Having thus united their forces, the Lenape and Mengwe declared war against the Alligewi, and great battles were fought, in which many warriors fell on both sides. The enemy fortified their large towns and erected fortifications, especially on large rivers, and near lakes, where they were successively attacked and sometimes stormed by the allies. An engagement took place in which hundreds fell, who were afterwards buried in holes or laid together in heaps and covered over with earth. No quarter was given, so that the Alligewi, at last, finding that their destruction was inevitable if they persisted in their obstinacy, abandoned the country to the conquerors, and fled down the Mississippi river, from whence they never returned. The war which was carried on with this nation, lasted many years, during which the Lenape lost a great number of their warriors, while the Mengwe would always hang back in the rear, leaving them to face the enemy. In the end, the conquerors divided the country between themselves; the Mengwe made choice of the lands in the vicinity of the great lakes, and on their tributary streams, and the Lenape took possession of the country to the south.

While it is acknowledged that war may have played a role in the abandonment of Cahokia, other factors may also have contributed to its downfall. Climate change, with a lack of rainfall, over-exploitation of resources, flooding, earthquakes, and others, have all been argued as reasons for the abandonment of Cahokia by the 1300s. In any case, the Mississippian culture represented by Cahokia spread to several tribes. Today, the Osages, the Chickasaws, and the Peorias all claim they are descendants of the Cahokia.

Chapter Two

Iroquois Wars

The Illinois (Illini) Indians are the first primary inhabitants of Illinois for whom we have first-hand information. The French-Canadian voyageurs who traded knives, kettles, beads, and other goods with them for furs provided this information. Their original reports began in the late 1630s and after placed the Illinois south of Lake Michigan and said they were near and continually warred with the Sioux tribe. Frenchmen such as the missionary Jean-Claude Allouez, the trader and government official Nicholas Perrot, and others beginning in the 1660s, wrote of their contacts with the Illinois. Allouez had made the first known contact with the Illinois Indians in the mid-1650s on the south shore of Lake Superior at Chequamegon Bay.

The Illinois belonged to the Algonquian linguistic family. These tribes dwelled from the Rocky Mountains to the Atlantic Ocean and Newfoundland to Tennessee. According to Illinois legend, they originally came from a distant sea to the west. The Illinois settled in a bountiful land full of game: Deer, elk, wolves, bears, wild turkeys, and other game abounded. The Illinois Indians even hunted buffalo, which did not disappear from the state of Illinois until the early nineteenth century. The Illinois lived in cabins made from saplings bent over and then covered with reed mats and bark from twelve feet in length. Thinking themselves superior to other Indians, the Illinois referred to themselves as Iliniwek, meaning "the men," the French described them as tall and all-built.

The Illinois were the most numerous Indians who inhabited the present state of Illinois at the time of first contact with the French. The loose Illinois confederacy consisted of six primary tribes: Kaskaskia, Peoria, Cahokia, Tamaroa, Moingwena, and Michigamea. Other minor bands were the Korakoenitanon, Chinko, Tapouro, Omouachoa, Chepoussa (spellings of the various tribes vary), and a few others. While their central location was in Illinois, they ranged east to the Miami and Ohio rivers, north to the Fox River in Wisconsin, west of the Mississippi, and south to Arkansas. They were closely related to the Miami, who spoke the same language and resided in the Chicago region.

According to the Jesuit Missionary Gabriel Druilletes, in 1667-1668 the Illinois had sixty villages with a population of 100,000-120,000, including 20,000 warriors. By 1680, internal warfare with the Sioux, Winnebago, and Iroquois had reduced their population to approximately 10,000. Though the numbers given by Druillete are probably exaggerated, the Illinois did suffer a significant population loss during those years. Among the several reasons for this vast population loss was their long war against the Sioux. A second incident involved the Winnebago sometime before contact with the French. The Illinois sent five hundred men to aid the Winnebago, who had suffered from attacks by the Ottawa and a plague. In an act of almost unbelievable treachery, considering the circumstances, the Winnebago slaughtered the Illinois during a dance held in their village. In retaliation, the Illinois assembled a large war party and attacked the Winnebago in the middle of the winter. The Illinois waited until the ice froze, allowing them easy access to the island retreat where the Winnebago had sought a haven. The Illinois killed all but one hundred to one hundred-fifty of the Winnebago but incurred heavy losses. During this period the Illinois also engaged in continuous warfare with the Osages and the Chickasaws to the south.

The war with the Iroquois Confederacy was a third cause of the vast loss of the Illinois population. The Iroquois Confederacy comprised the Mohawk, Cayuga, Onondaga, Oneida, and the Seneca. The Iroquois initiated war with the Illinois as they expanded west to keep them and other tribes from trading furs to the French. The Iroquois desired furs to trade to the Dutch in Albany (New York) and then with the English after their conquest of New Netherland in 1664. There, they traded furs for firearms, knives, axes, kettles, and other trade goods they desired. By the 1640s, the Iroquois had depleted the sought-after beaver in their homeland, Northern New York. Beginning about 1641, the Iroquois instigated wars against their neighbors to obtain furs for themselves. Subsequently, the Iroquois attacked and defeated other nations in their vicinity, including the Hurons, Erie, and Neutrals, in the 1640s and 1650s. As the fur trade moved further north along the St. Lawrence River, they attacked the Ottawa. They pushed other tribes further west into Wisconsin, including the Potawatomi, Fox, Mascouten, and Miami. These tribes settled around Green Bay, which became the center of the fur trade in the region.

Meanwhile, the Illinois began bringing their furs to Wisconsin to trade. According to Perrot, in 1655-1656, a war party of Iroquois attacked an Illinois village and killed the women and children. The Illinois organized a pursuit, surprised the Iroquois, and killed most of them. The Illinois also killed Iroquois hunting for beaver in their territory. In addition to the Illinois fur trade with the French, these attacks on Iroquois hunters begged Iroquois retaliation for the interference in their fur acquisition efforts. Thus, starting in the mid-1650s, war raged between the Illinois and the Iroquois. The fierce Iroquois attacks forced most of the Illinois to retreat west of the Mississippi River.

After the Iroquois attacks decreased, the Illinois returned to their homeland in the early 1670s. In 1673, Jacques Marquette found the Illinois in a village of seventy-four cabins across the Illinois River from Starved Rock on his return from exploration of the Mississippi River with Louis Jolliet. When Allouez visited the town in 1677, it had grown to three hundred and seventy-three cabins and had a population of over 5000. During this period, the Illinois were at war simultaneously with the Fox near Green Bay and also the Iroquois, who were sending out war parties against them.

The explorer and fur trader Rene' Robert Cavalier, Sieur de La Salle, entered Illinois in 1679 to establish a French fur trading post there. La Salle built Fort Creve Coeur, a small enclosure twenty-five feet high enclosing a cabin and a few barracks, in January 1680, about a mile down the Illinois River from Peoria Lake. La Salle left his lieutenant Henri de Tonti in command when he departed for Fort Frontenac. He warned the men that the Iroquois might attack the Illinois soon. While on his journey up the Illinois River, La Salle sent Tonti a message advising him to seek refuge at Starved Rock across the river, the large Illinois village of La Vantum, if the Iroquois attacked. After most of the men deserted, Tonti abandoned the fort with two priests and three men and traveled upriver to join the Illinois Indians. At the time, about 7000 or 8000 Illinois were residing there.

That summer, Tonti recorded the first battles between the Iroquois and the Illinois observed by the French in 1680. In August 1680, a scout rode into the Illinois village to warn them that a large party of Iroquois (five hundred to six hundred Iroquois and one hundred Shawnee) was nearby. Nehemiah Matson wrote an eighteenth-century version of the battle.

Nehemiah Matson (1816-1873) was a local amateur historian who lived in Princeton, Illinois, after 1836, near the Illinois River and Starved Rock. He also researched early French narratives in France that would later be published in the "Jesuit Relations." The following battle account is taken from his book *French and Indians of the Illinois River, published in 1874.*

The Alarm and Preparation For Defense

It was near the close of a warm day in the latter part of August, 1680, when a scout arrived with his horse in a foam of sweat, and shouting at the top of his voice that the Iroquois were marching against the town. All was now excitement and confusion; squaws screamed, papooses quit their plays on the green, and ran away to their homes; warriors caught their weapons and made preparations to defend their town and protect their squaws and little ones. During the night fires were kept burning along the river bank, and every preparation made to defend the town in case it should be attacked The warriors greased their bodies, painted their faces red, and ornamented their heads with turkey feathers; war songs were sung, drums beat; warriors dance, yelled and brandished their war clubs to keep up their courage. At last morning came, and with it the savage Iroquois.

When news came of the approaching Iroquois, a crowd of excited savages collected around Tonti and his companions, whom they had previously suspected of treachery, and charged them with being in league with their enemies. A report having reached them that a number of Jesuit priests, and even La Salle himself was with the Iroquois, and leading them on to the town. The enraged warriors seized the blacksmith forge, tools, and all the goods that belonged to the French, and threw them into the river. One of the warriors caught Tonti by the hair of his head and raised his tomahawk to split his skull, but a friendly chief caught the savage by the arm, and his life was spared. Tonti, with that boldness and self-possession which was characteristic of him, defended himself against these charges, and in order to convince them of his good faith, offered to accompany them to battle.

Father Gabriel and Zenobe were away at their altar, spending the day in prayer and meditation, and had no warning of the danger that awaited them. On their return home late at night, they were surprised to find the town in a whirlpool of excitement; squaws were crying and bewailing their fate, while the warriors were dancing, yelling and offering up sacrifices to the Manito of battle.

On arrival of the two priests; the savages collected around them, charging them with treachery, and being the cause of the Iroquois invading their country. The priests, with uplifted hands, called God to witness their innocence of the charge, but their statement did not change the minds of the excited Indians. A loud clamor was raised for their blood, and a number of warriors sprang forward with uplifted tomahawks to put an end to their existence, but as they drew nigh and were about to tomahawk them, Father Gabriel drew from his bosom a small gold image of the Holy Virgin, and held it up before their would-be executioners. On seeing this sacred talisman the Indians paused a moment, and then returned their tomahawks to their belts. Father Zenobe afterwards said this was another proof to the Virgin protecting the Jesuits in North America.

During the night all the squaws and pappooses, with the old Indians unable to bear arms, were placed in canoes and taken down the river about three leagues, to a large marshy island. About sixty warriors were left for their protection, and all of them secreted themselves in the reeds and high grass, so they could not be seen by the Iroquois. But the sequel shows that they did not escape the vigilance of the enemy, and this island of supposed safety became their tomb.

The Battle and Massacre

At La Vantum during the Iroquois invasion, there were only about five hundred warriors at La Vantum (other authors state only a few hundred). The head chief, Chassagoac, and a large portion of his braves had gone to Cahokia for the purpose of attending a religious feast. But this band, small as it was, boldly crossed the river at daylight, and met the enemy, whose number was five times as large as their own. While they were ascending the bluff, a scout met them saying that the enemy were crossing the prairie between the Vermillion and Illinois timber. As the invaders approached the river timber, they were surprised to meet the Illinoisans, who were lying in ambush, and received them with a deadly fire. At this unexpected attack, the Iroquois were stricken with a panic and fled from the field, leaving the ground covered with the dead and wounded. But they soon rallied and the fight became bloody, arrows and rifle balls flying thick and fast, while the woods far and near resounded with the wild whoops of contending savages.

In the midst of the flight, Tonti undertook the perilous task of mediating between the contending parties. Laying aside his gun and taking a wampum belt in his hand, holding it over his head as a flag of truce, and amid showers of arrows and bullets, he walked boldly forward to meet the enemy. As he approached, the Iroquois warriors collected around him in a threatening manner, one of whom attempted to stab him to the heart, but the knife striking a rib inflicted only a long, shallow gash. As the savage was about to repeat the blow a chief came up, and seeing he was a white man, protected him from further assault, and applied a bandage to the wound to stop its bleeding. The fighting having ceased, a warrior took Tonti's hat, and placing it on the muzzle of his gun, started toward the Illinoisans, who, on seeing it, supposed he was killed and again renewed the fight. While the battle was in progress, a warrior reported that three Frenchmen, armed with guns, were with the Illinois forces, and firing on them. When this announcement was made the Iroquois became enraged at Tonti, and again gathered around him, some for killing and others for his protection. One of the warriors caught him by the hair of his head, raising it up, and with his long knife was about to take off his scalp, when Tonti, with his iron hand, knocked down his assailant. Others attacked Tonti with knives and tomahawks, but he was again rescued from death by the head-chief.

For a long time the battle raged, many of the combatants on both sides being slain, and the yells of the warriors could be heard far away. But at last the Illinoisans, whose force was inferior to their adversary, were overpowered and driven from the field. The vanquished fled to their town, with the intention of defending it or perish in the attempt.

On the river bank, near the center of the town was their great council-house, surrounded by stockades, forming a kind of fortification. To this the remnant of the warriors fled, and in great haste tore down the lodges and used the material in strengthening their works.

The Illinoisans had crossed the river in canoes, but their pursuers having no means of crossing at this point, were obliged to go up to the rapids where they forded it. In a short time the Iroquois attacked the town, setting fire to the lodges and fortifications, which were soon a mass of flames. Many of the besieged were burned in their strongholds, others were slain or taken prisoners as they escaped from the flames; a few only succeeded in the preservation of their lives by escaping down the river. The town, with the great council-house and fortifications, was destroyed by fire, and nothing was left of them except the blackened poles which the lodges were constructed.

When the victory was completed they bound the prisoners hand and foot, and commenced torturing them to make them reveal the hiding place of their squaws and papooses.

On obtaining the necessary information a large war party took the canoes left by the vanquished Illinoisans, and descended the river in search of the squaws and papooses. While these defenseless beings were secreted among the reeds and high grass of the island, they were discovered by the savage Iroquois, and all of them slain. The sixty warriors left to guard them fled on the approach of the enemy, crossing the lake and secreting themselves in the thick river timber.

Torturing the Prisoners

On the following day after the battle, the victors made preparations to torture the prisoners; and their acts of barbarity probably never have been equaled by any savages of the west. The warriors were formed into a large circle, and the prisoners, bound hand and foot, were converted thither, when the work of torture commenced. The doomed prisoners were seated on the ground awaiting their fate, some of whom were weeping or praying, while others were engaged in singing their death song. A warrior, with a long knife, cut off the nose and ears of the prisoners, and threw them to their hungry dogs. Pieces of flesh were cut out of their arms and breasts, while the prisoners sat writhing with agony; and the ground around them red with human gore. The work of torture went on--the executioners continued to cut off limbs and pieces of flesh-and in some cases the bowels were taken out and trailed on the ground, while the groans and screams of the victims in their death agonies were terrible to witness.

Tonti and his companions looked on these barbarous acts of the Iroquois with horror and astonishment, but dare not remonstrate as they were prisoners also, and did not know but a like fate awaited them.

While the torture was going on the two priests were engaged in baptizing the victims, in order to absolve them from past sins, and as each one was about to expire, they would hold the crucifix before his eyes, so he might look on it, and through its divine efficacy his soul would be saved from perdition

When the prisoners were all dead, the warriors cut out their hearts, roasted and eat them in order to make them brave.

For a number of days the Iroquois continued to rejoice over their victory, spending the time in singing and dancing around the scalps, and causing the timber and river bluffs to re-echo with their yells and wild whoops.

Death of Father Gabriel

Two days after the Iroquois victory, the French were set at liberty, and they departed in an old leaky canoe. After going about six leagues, they stopped at the mouth of a large creek to repair the canoe and dry their clothing. While thus engaged, Father Gabriel, who was always fond of solitude, wandered off into the thick river timber for the purpose of prayer and meditation. When the canoe was repaired, clothes dried, and time of departure came, Father Gabriel was missing, and they searched for him among the thick timber, but he could not be found. During the night fires were kept burning along the river bank, and guns discharged to direct him to camp, but all in vain. During the following day they searched the woods far and near for the missing priest, and Father Zenobe prayed to the Holy Virgin for his safe return, but all to no purpose, so they gave him up for lost, and continued their journey. For many days they mourned the loss of the holy father, as he was an old man of nearly three score years, and devoted to the work of the church.

It was afterwards ascertained that Father Gabriel was taken prisoner by the Indians, carried to their camp some miles off, where he was executed, and while his friends were searching for him those savages were dancing around his scalp.

While Father Gabriel was at prayer in the thick timber, some distance from his companions, he was approached by two Indians in a threatening manner. With his head uncovered he arose to meet them, with one hand pointing heavenward and the other to the gold cross on his breast giving them to understand that he was a priest. In vain he told them that he was their friend, and had come from afar across the big waters to teach them in the ways of truth and happiness. Regardless of his entreaties, they bound his hands behind his back and led him off a prisoner to their camp. A council was held over the captives and it was decided that he should die. A stake was driven into the ground, and Father Gabriel with his hands and feet pinioned, tied to it. Here, he sat on the ground bound to the stake, with his long hair and flowing beard white with the snows of seventy winters, waving to and fro in the wind. The Indians formed a circle around their victim, singing and dancing while flourishing their war-clubs over his head, and occasionally yelling at the top of their voices. This performance continued for some time, while the victim sat with his head bowed down, his eyes fixed on the gold cross which hung on his breast, and in silence awaited his doom.

Under repeated blows of war-clubs, Father Gabriel fell to the ground and soon expired. His clothing and scalp were taken off by the savages, and his remains left to be devoured by the wolves.

La Salle's Return

About three months after the Iroquois had massacred the Illinois Indians, La Salle and his party returned from Canada to attend to his colony. When they reached the site of La Vantum, they only saw the destroyed charred remains of the once vibrant village. They were greeted only by partially decomposed skulls and bones and mangled bodies scattered over the grounds. Tonti and his companions were nowhere to be found. Afterward, they traveled further downriver in search of further clues to what happened to their companions. They did not discover their companions but did find the remains of the Indians whom the Iroquois had tortured and killed on an island.

Most of the Illinois Indians had fled down the Illinois River. The Iroquois followed, camping on one side of the river and the Illinois on the other. When the Illinois reached the mouth of the Illinois River, the Iroquois told them there would be peace now that the Illinois had vacated their homeland. The Iroquois promised to leave them if the Illinois would disperse and refrain from any more hostile actions. Most of the Illinois then crossed the Mississippi River. However, the Tamaroa stayed on the Illinois side of the Mississippi River. The treacherous Iroquois then attacked and killed about 1200 Tamaroa.

The other tribes fled across the Mississippi River and lived with Osages, and some even sought refuge with the Fox up north. One chief of the Kaskaskia, Paessa, who at the time of the massacre had been away hunting, upon his return with a hundred warriors, took up the trail of the Iroquois and engaged them in battle but were repelled. They failed to rescue the seven hundred Illinois captives whom the Iroquois burned at the stake when they returned home. Paessa was killed in the battle. However, the remaining warriors continued to pursue Iroquois hunting parties throughout the winter of 1681 in the Lake Erie region. After this thrashing by the Iroquois, the Illinois tribes would never ultimately reign over the Illinois region again.

The Iroquois released Tonti and forced him to leave the region. He later rejoined La Salle at Mackinac. After traveling down to the mouth of the Mississippi River, La Salle returned to Illinois. Fearing that the Iroquois would again return to Illinois, he and Tonti built Fort St. Louis at Starved Rock in December 1682. They constructed a storehouse for pelts and residences for the men and surrounded the summit with a fifteen-foot-high palisade. Starved Rock, which got its name later due to the tradition that enemies assaulting Illinois Indians starved a group of them there, was a natural rocky fortress encompassing about half an acre on a bluff one hundred and twenty-five feet above the Illinois River. The natural fortress was inaccessible on three sides and easily defended on the one remaining side with difficult access.

To defend against the Iroquois, La Salle worked to confederate the various tribes in the region. About two hundred Shawnee and 1300 Miami, closely related to the Illinois, and various other tribes settled near the fort until there were nearly 4000 warriors among the 20,000 Indians. La Salle left in August 1683 and again left Tonti in command of fifty French soldiers and about one hundred Indian allies.

A Second Iroquois attack on La Vantum

In May 1684, the Iroquois attacked La Vantum again. The following account of the battle is Matson's.

> It was a bright clear day in the latter part of May, and the great meadow was green with grass, intermixed with flowers of various hues; the trees were in full leaf: and the air was fragrant with blossoms of the wild plum and crabapple; birds were singing among the branches of trees, and squirrels chirping in the thick river timber, while at a distance was heard the sweet notes of the robin and meadow lark. In the shade of the willows and elms on the river bank lay the doe and her fawn, lulled to slumber by the hum of the wild bee and grasshopper.
>
> All was quiet at Fort St. Louis, and inmates were delighted with the beauty of the surrounding scenery. To the west, in plain view, lay the great town of La Vantum, with its many hundred lodges built along the bank of the river, and around which

were collected thousands of human beings. On the race track, above the town, warriors mounted on ponies were practicing horsemanship, while far in the distance squaws were seen engaged in planting com or gathering greens for their family meal.

It was Sabbath morning, the fourth after Easter; all the inmates of Port St. Louis were dressed in their best apparel, and seated under the shade of cedars, awaiting religious services. Father Zenobe, dressed in his long black robe, with a large gold cross hanging from his neck, was about to commence services, when a lone Indian was seen on the bottom prior going westward, and urging his pony forward at the top of its speed.

Father Zenobe after concluding his sermon, was about to administer the sacrament, when the sentinel at the gate fired his gun to give an alarm. At this signal the meeting broke up, and everyone ran to his post, thinking that the fort was about to be attacked. On looking in the direction of the town everything appeared in commotion. Warriors mounted on ponies were riding back and forth at full gallop, squaws and pappooses running hither and thither in wild confusion; drums beating, warriors yelling, while the cries and lamentations of the frightened people could be heard even at the fort. Tonti, with three companions, came down from the fort, boarded a canoe, and with all haste proceeded down the river to ascertain the cause of this excitement, and upon his arrival the mystery was explained.

A scout had arrived with the intelligence that a large body of Iroquois were only ten leagues distant and marching on the town. The tragedy of four years previous was fresh in their minds, and fearing a like result caused them to go wild with terror. The chiefs and warriors collected around

Tonti, beseeching him to protect them from the scalping knives and tomahawks of their enemies, in accordance with La Salle's promise. Tonti, in reply, said that his force was not sufficient to afford them protection but advised them to collect their warriors and defend the town. The French, who lived in the town with their wives and a few Indian friends, fled to the fort for security, but the warriors, being seized with a panic and fearing another massacre, in great haste fled, some going down the river in canoes, while others mounted their ponies and galloped westward across the country. Soon after their departure the invaders came, two thousand strong, but they found a barren victory, as not one living soul was left in La Vantum. (Other authors state the Iroquois force was only about two hundred).

When the Iroquois found their intended victims had fled, they attacked the fort and held it in siege six days. For a number of days the Indians continued to fire on the fort from a neighboring cli but without producing any effect. The fort not returning the fire, emboldened the assailants, and each day they came closer, and occupied the timber near the base of the rock, with the intention, no doubt, of making an assault. But when they were in close range, the guns were brought to bear on them, and they received the fire of both muskets and cannon. Many were killed, others wounded, while the survivors, being stricken with panic, fled in great haste, leaving their dead and wounded behind.

Aftermath of the Iroquois Wars

After repulsing the attack, the French remained in the fort for many days and did not leave until they were persuaded that the Iroquois had gone. The Illinois pursued the Iroquois and inflicted some losses. The French and Indian allies, including the Ottawa, Huron, Mississauga, and Ojibwa, went on the offensive against the Iroquois in the latter 1680s and defeated them in several battles. They brazenly invaded Iroquois lands, bolstered by their victories, burning four Seneca villages in 1686 and Onondaga village in 1696. Illinois Indians joined these efforts. In 1687, two hundred Illinois warriors accompanied Tonti to Canada and joined the army of Governor Denonville in an expedition against the Iroquois. Again, in 1688, eight hundred Illinois warriors journeyed east to join the French against the Iroquois. Tonti continued to send out Illinois Indians against the Iroquois after 1693. The Illinois brought back scalps, a total of over four hundred Iroquois men, women, and children, before the Iroquois made peace with the French in 1701. The Iroquois managed some raids into Illinois in the 1690s, and one last raid was reported in 1714.

Chapter Three

Fox Wars

The Fox tribe (called Mesquakie, Renards (Fox) by the French and known as Outagami by the Chippewa and Huron inhabited Eastern Wisconsin in the Green Bay region and along the Fox and Wisconsin rivers. While most Western tribes were allies of the French, the Fox became opposed to the French when they started trading muskets to their enemies, the Sioux, beginning in 1679 and the early 1680s. They sometimes plundered French traders as they traveled the Fox and Wisconsin Rivers to trade with the Sioux, who were becoming more potent due to the influx of French arms. During the 1690s, the Fox and their allies, the Mascouten, raided and fought the Sioux. Meanwhile, French hostility toward the Fox intensified as their Iroquois enemies attempted to draw them into the British trade sphere.

French hostility towards the Fox erupted into war in the decade after Antoine de la Mothe Cadillac founded Detroit in 1701 and built Fort Pontchartrain. He tried to draw various tribes to settle there to trade their furs instead of trading with Frenchmen in distant locations. Two Fox villages moved there in the winter of 1710-11 to be closer to the British and simultaneously further away from the enemy Sioux. In 1712, Ottawas and Potawatomi attacked the Mascouten, allies of the Fox, who then fled to the nearby Fox camp. Believing that the French had aided their enemies, the Potawatomi and the Ottawas, the Fox surrounded and besieged the French fort. The current French commander, Jacques Charles Renard Dubuisson, summoned their allies, the Ottawas, the Potawatomi, the

Hurons, and the Illinois Confederacy. The Illinois chief Makouandeby joined the anti-Fox tribes surrounding and besieging the Fox. After a three-week siege, the Fox broke out during a thunderstorm. They were chased down by their enemies, who proceeded to slaughter almost a thousand of them. The Fox survivors who reached their homeland broadcasted the details of their ordeal, and what had been called the Fox Wars began.

Before 1712, there had been enmity between the Fox, Mascouten, and Sauk tribes against the Illinois tribes. In the early 1700s, Mascouten and Wisconsin Kickapoo hunters began trespassing on northern Illinois territory. An Illinois war party fought against Fox and Mascouten in 1712. However, hostilities were carried on to a new intensity after the slaughter of the Fox in Detroit.

In the aftermath of the slaughter at Detroit, Fox Chief Kiala built a confederacy of Sioux, Iowa, Mascouten, Kickapoo, Sauk, Winnebago, and Western Abenaki against the French and their Illinois allies. Previously, the Fox had been at war with the Sioux. They made peace with them, which freed their warriors to turn against the French and the Illinois Indians in earnest. In 1713-1714, the Fox raided Illinois near Peoria and killed or carried off seventy-seven of the Illinois. The French forged a confederation of Indians against the Fox in 1714 to exterminate them. In 1715, a force of four hundred Illinois warriors, in conjunction with Hurons and other Indians from Detroit, killed an estimated one hundred Fox warriors and took forty-seven prisoners in a battle probably on the Fox River. Again, in 1718, a large war party invaded the Illinois River area. From that time forward, the Fox regularly conducted attacks on Illinois villages. The Fox allies, the Kickapoo, who had absorbed the remaining Mascouten, had also been slaughtered in the siege. They also never ceased to be bitter enemies of the Illinois. In 1718, the Kickapoo moved from Wisconsin into Illinois and established villages along the Rock River, during which time the

Kickapoo fought the Illinois and drove them further south. Several skirmishes took place in 1719 between the Fox and the Illinois, one in which a Fox hunting party killed over twenty Illinois. In 1721, the Fox raided deep into Southern Illinois as far south as Kaskaskia. In this particular expedition, the Fox were repulsed by the Illinois, who then pursued them and succeeded in inflicting many casualties. They captured over thirty Fox warriors with the assistance of several couriers de bois. The captives were given to the Peoria, who then tortured and burned them.

Unfortunately for the Illinois, one of the captives was Minchilay, a nephew of the Fox chief Ouchala. The following year, the vengeful Ouchala led a vast war party to those responsible for the deed, the Peoria village at Pimitoui at the outlet of Lake Peoria. Nevertheless, before the Fox invasion, the Peoria had taken refuge at Starved Rock, joining with some of their members already there. The Fox attacked, killing at least four Illinois, and then surrounded and besieged those who had fled to the top of Starved Rock, where they could defend themselves but could not escape. After an indefinite time, under the duress of hunger and thirst, the Illinois attempted to negotiate with the Fox. Though he had set out to destroy the Illinois, for some reason, perhaps fear of French reprisals Ouchala agreed to release the Illinois from their deathtrap under the condition that they would return all their Fox, Kickapoo, and Mascouten prisoners. The Illinois gratefully agreed and quickly retreated down to Southern Illinois. Ouchala then traveled to Green Bay to explain his actions to Monsieur de Montigny, the fort commander. There, Ouchala declared the war was over and that the Fox would not attack anyone unless they were attacked. However, he did not speak for the whole tribe. The Fox attacked the Illinois three times near Fort Chartres in 1722.

In 1723, a Fox band tried to settle themselves at Starved Rock. The Illinois sent out a war party of two hundred to remove them. However, the Fox repelled the attack, killing eleven of the warriors. The Fox, then embittered because the Illinois had not returned capturd prisoners, raided Southern Illinois close to Fort Chartres. In 1714 and 1725, the Fox, Kickapoo, and Mascouten raided so frequently that even French residents of the American bottom could not plant or cultivate their crops. These raids interrupted the fur trade so much that Illinois officials reported that no furs would be brought to market as long as the war with the Fox lasted. In 1725, Illinois leaders submitted a list of almost a hundred of their kin that had been killed in Fox raids in the previous ten years.

    Also in 1725, a delegation of Indians, including Chicagou (Chicago), a chief of the Michigamea, traveled to France. While there, he complained of Fox depredations and pled for French assistance. The French court ordered the governor of New France, Monsieur de Vaudreuil, to end the conflict and stop any further hostilities by the Fox. The Fox learned that the new French Governor Charles de la Boisch, Marquis de Beaucharnois, had made plans in 1727 to send an expedition against them in 1728. In 1728, the Fox again invaded Illinois and were struck near Chicago by a force of several hundred Illinois and twenty French. The same year, Constant Le Marchand de Lignery, a force of 1650 French and Indians, marched on the Fox villages near Lake Winnebago, which the Fox had abandoned in anticipation of an attack. Lignery burned the dwellings and crops and withdrew.

    The French achieved a coup against the Fox when, in 1727, they persuaded the Sioux to break their peace agreement with them. In addition to renewed hostilities with the Sioux, the Fox warriors performed several foolish actions to antagonize their remaining allies. In one instance, a young Fox war party angered the Kickapoo and Mascouten by killing a few of their hunters after one band of Kickapoos refused to turn over some Frenchmen to them. In another incident, the Fox turned against the Winnebago when they refused to turn over a few men who had guided a party of Ottawa, Menominee, and Chippewa against them. By 1730, even the Winnebago, the last of the Fox allies, opposed them.

The Fox Destruction

Surrounded by enemies, isolated without any allies, and knowing the French were determined to exterminate them, in May of 1730, the Fox leadership met to discuss a plan of action. Believing they were no longer safe in Wisconsin, they sought permission from the Iroquois to settle on their land. In June, many Fox decided to make the eight-hundred-mile journey away from their homelands to join the Iroquois. This would set the stage for a battle in Illinois territory that would essentially destroy the Fox.

Once most of the Fox (about six hundred stayed in Wisconsin) decided to emigrate east, they planned to travel south to Stared Rock first and then to turn east across the Illinois prairie. By taking this route, they hoped to avoid their strong and dangerous enemies, the Potawatomi, Ottawa, and Hurons, who occupied the territory adjacent to the Southern tip of Lake Michigan. In central Illinois, only the weak Illinois Confederacy could hinder them. The Fox thought the Illinois were a minor obstacle that could quickly be dealt with, and in any case, they were hoping to avoid meeting them altogether. In early June, approximately 1300 Fox, including between two hundred and three hundred warriors, set out for their destination in New York.

Through several Mascouten and Kickapoo married to Fox women, the French learned of Fox's planned intentions, but did not take the report seriously. The Fox moved unhindered to a campsite not far from the Fox and Illinois River junction, where they rested, needed clothes, made new moccasins, and hunted to restock their food supply. Regrettably for the Fox, their hunters encountered and skirmished with Cahokia hunters. During the skirmish, the Fox captured seventeen of their enemies. However, the Cahokia hunters who escaped warned their fellow tribesman at their recently established village near Starved Rock, only fifteen miles away from the Fox campsite.

The Fox had not expected to find members of the Illinois Confederacy near Starved Rock. The Fox leaders sent a delegation to the Cahokia village to avoid the chance that the Illinois might summon additional allies, which could thwart a peaceful journey. During a hostile council with the Cahokia elders, the Fox representatives negotiated the captive's return in exchange for noninterference in their journey east. Amid the negotiations, one angry Cahokia warrior armed with a hunting knife suddenly leaped toward a Fox delegate and stabbed him. Enraged at this breach of protocol, the Fox broke off negotiations with the knowledge that the Cahokia had already dispatched runners to Kickapoo and Mascouten in the area.

In a bitter rage, the Fox reacted to the fruitless negotiations with the antagonistic Illinois by foolishly torturing and burning to death their Illinois captives, including the son of a paramount chief. Fox scouts soon informed their leaders that enemy Kickapoo and Mascouten were approaching them from the northwest. Realizing the dangerous predicament that they were now in, the Fox broke camp in late July, headed south, and then turned east across the Grand Prairie of Illinois. Hoping to escape their enemies before they knew their plan, but weighed down by children and the elderly, the Fox move slowly toward the Wabash River.

However, Cahokia scouts kept a close eye on their movements. While the Cahokia did not have enough manpower to overpower or block the Fox, they attempted to slow down their progress. Cahokia harassment could only buy time for reinforcements to arrive. Cahokia warriors caught the Fox in a vulnerable position when, on August 4, they were fording the Sangamon River in current

Mac Clean County in central Illinois. Realizing that their women and children were especially susceptible to enemy fire, the Fox responded to their predicament by encamping in a small grove of trees by a river. The Fox then attempted to engage the Cahokia in battle. Instead, the Cahokia would retreat briefly when the Fox charged. The Fox would return to their camp, and the Cahokia would advance again. This seesaw skirmish continued for hours until the Fox noticed a large war party of almost two hundred Potawatomi, Kickapoo, and Mascouten warriors advancing toward them in the reinforcement of the Cahokia.

Suddenly, the irritating harassment of the Cahokia had morphed into a severe fatal threat to the Fox's survival. The Fox quickly broke off their attack and switched to a defensive position. The Potawatomi war chiefs Maudoche and Okia, now in conjunction with the Cahokia, soon assaulted the Fox defensive perimeter from two sides. Protected by the trees, the Fox repelled the attacks in fighting that lasted well into the evening. During this initial clash, the Fox lost seven killed and thirty wounded. The Potawatomi and their allies lost a similar number, including Chief Okia's death, while the Cahokia's losses are unknown.

Pondering their options that night after a few unsuccessful attempts to break out of their encampment, the Fox chiefs decided to fortify their position. Their enemies were out in the surrounding open prairie, which extended for miles around their small grove of trees. Fox hunters had recently brought in several deer and bison and had ample powder and lead. The Fox did not think their enemies would linger for a siege because they would soon deplete the food resources in the nearby area needed to maintain an army. Therefore, they decided to fortify their position and began to cut down trees to build houses and a barrier.

The Fox dug out the earth two to three feet deep and constructed tiny oval-shaped houses about three feet wide and six feet long covered with a roof of reed mats and dirt to make them bulletproof. They also heaped up the soil a few feet high, topped by a wooden palisade extending on three sides, making a fort approximately one hundred feet by three hundred and fifty feet long. In addition, for further protection, they piled up branches on the perimeter to hide from enemy observation and dug shallow trenches around the perimeter and from shelter to shelter. Finally, they dug trenches covered with reed mats on the side bound by the river to provide protected access to water. Understandably, with all their fortification efforts and seemingly sufficient supplies, the Fox thought they could withstand enemy assaults and survive a short siege.

The hitherto undaunted Fox soon experienced the determination of their opponents to destroy them. They were severely disappointment when enemy reinforcements arrived on August 17. Cahokia runners had brought news of the Fox flight to other tribes of the Illinois Confederacy in the vicinity of Fort de Chartres. Almost immediately, three hundred Illinois warriors departed to join their brethren surrounding the Fox. The Fort commander, Robert Groston de St. Ange, soon departed with about one hundred French soldiers and traders and another one hundred Illinois warriors. On the way, St. Ange's party joined the previous group of three hundred warriors, and they all arrived at the Fox Fort together.

August 17th would be a disastrous day for the Fox, significantly increasing the odds against them. Nicoles-Antoine Coulon de Villiers arrived with approximately three hundred Sauk, Potawatomi, and Miami that day. Villiers had also been notified of the Fox entrapment. He had left Fort St. Joseph (present Niles, Michigan) on August 10th, the same day St. Ange had begun his march. Unbelievably, on the same day, Simon Reaume, a veteran trader at Fort Quiatenon (present-day Lafayette, Indiana), arrived with four hundred Wea and Piankashaw. Their arrival proved especially heartbreaking to the Fox as they had recently sent a few emissaries to the Wea, who had agreed to assist the Fox in their escape. When he heard of this, Reaume quickly persuaded the Wea to turn against their friends and relatives.

The Fox first attempted to negotiate with the French leaders to allow them to continue their journey to join the Senecas. Rejected by the French leadership, the Fox returned most of their remaining Illinois captives and proposed a surrender whereby their members would be divided among the various tribes. They hoped that this sacrifice would persuade the French to make peace. Instead, the French viewed the offer as a ruse to provide a means for the Fox to escape later. Also, the French believed that Fox's presence among the various tribes would influence them against the French. The Fox then slyly approached their former friends, the Sauk and Wea, appealing to their many kinship ties. They convinced the Sauk and Wea to harbor many of their children amongst themselves to keep them safe. During the siege, the Fox threw about three hundred children over the fortifications to obtain mercy. The Fox also hoped that if they escaped, parents could reunite themselves with their children. This action would also reduce their numbers and lessen the drain on the food supplies.

The alert Illinois detected Sauk and Wea's adoption of the Fox children, and they warned the French leadership that the Sauk and Weas were planning on assisting the Fox in escaping. To prevent any assistance from the Sauk and Weas, the French increased pressure on the Fox by starting random firing on Fox's defensive lines. The French also increased pressure on the Fox positions. A rush by forces under DeVilliers up the bluff on the north side of the encampment enabled the French to take the high point dominating the plain that the Fox had used as a watchtower. The French began to dig a trench towards the

Fox fort and built two towers close to the Fox perimeter to fire down on the Fox defenders.

Though the two sides were presently stalemated, time was not on the side of the trapped Fox defenders. The once-thought-ample food supply of the Fox diminished by the day, and they suffered from close confinement in the uncomfortable heat and humidity of August. Fortunately, sympathetic Sauk and Wea smuggled some small quantities of food to them. In a rapidly deteriorating situation, desperate Fox leaders managed to negotiate again with French leaders through the intercession of some Sauk. However, the French showed no pity even though the Fox had brought several infants. The French refused any negotiation compromise and even shot at the Fox under a flag of truce as they returned to their lines.

Even worse for the Fox, on September 1, another party of two hundred Potawatomi, Hurons, and Miami entered enemy lines, increasing the besiegers to approximately 1400 and dashing the Fox hope that there were Iroquois warriors coming to their rescue. Despite several attacks on their besiegers, the Fox could not break through the enemy perimeter around them. On September 7, they desperately attacked one section held by the Illinois, sending about two hundred of them fleeing. Still, Kickapoo warriors quickly rushed in to turn the Fox back into their defenses. The Fox knew they could not hold out for much longer as they were already boiling moccasins and clothing for sustenance. Hunger also affected the French and Indian besiegers, who were reduced to eating their rawhide shields.

In final desperation, the Fox plead to their god, Wisaka. On the night of September 8, under instruction from their shamans, the Fox began drumming and chanting to their god for help. Two Fox warriors unsuccessfully tried to sweep their sacred wolf skin over the river (but it fell in) in the hope of creating a fog to mask an escape.

The next day, the Fox learned that two hundred

Illinois warriors had deserted from the French and Indian army surrounding them. Later that day, they spotted dark storm clouds approaching them from the Northwest. Before sunset, the storm arrived with such a downpour that even the Fox enemies were forced to take shelter. Knowing their enemies had abandoned their picket lines, the Fox seized the opportunity as their only hope for escape. In small groups, they started crossing the river carrying what they could personally hold. They planned to travel southwest from the Fort and then regroup, hoping the severe weather would obliterate their trail.

The French realized that the Fox were fleeing through the cries of Fox children on the move. One fleeing woman blundered into a French outpost. She subsequently revealed the Fox's intentions. Fearful of friendly fire in the stormy night and the possibility that some of their Indian allies, particularly the Potawatomi, might take advantage of the confusion and attack members of the hated Illinois confederacy. The French waited until daylight to pursue the fleeing Fox. Still friendly Sauk (to the Fox) pursued and captured some Fox Indians and brought them to their encampments for safety.

By daybreak, Many Fox fled about twelve miles southwest of the fort. At this time, Fox leaders gathered the various groups and pushed them onward, placing their warriors in the rear. By late morning, the enemy was seen approaching. The French and Indians quickly followed the Fox since their scouts had monitored the Fox flight during the night.

The Fox were low on ammunition due to the rainstorm dampening their gunpowder. They bravely formed a skirmish line, knowing they were almost certain to die while fighting against the overwhelming odds facing them. Approximately three hundred Fox warriors stood their ground and fought a short, fierce, and bloody battle against about 1200 foes, with only a little over fifty escaping the slaughter. Most of the women and children were soon overtaken. About three hundred of the Fox were killed, and the rest were made prisoners, with perhaps another three hundred dying under torture and burning.

Aftermath

In the years following the battle, the French attempted to completely destroy the Fox tribe in Wisconsin. However, some tribes, in particular the former friends of the Fox, the Sauk, Mascouten, and Kickapoo, reacted to the French genocidal policy by releasing their remaining Fox captives to return to their homeland. After further French attacks on the Fox in the early and mid-1730s, the significantly weakened Fox merged with the Sauk tribe.

From the 1730 battle with the Fox, the Illinois Confederation continued intermittent warfare inside and outside the state. These wars steadily depleted the numbers of Illinois Indians and weakened their capacity to maintain their dominance of Illinois territory. In the 1730s and early 1740s, the Illinois would skirmish against the Fox, Mascouten, and Sioux. Perhaps the most severe loss to the Illinois occurred in 1752 when a combined force of possibly 1000 Fox, Sioux, Sauk, and Kickapoo attacked the Michigamea, killed seventy to eighty members, and destroyed the village. This was in retaliation for the capture and burning of six Fox hunters by the Illinois during a time of peace.

The Illinois also fought against the Shawnee in Southern Illinois. The Shawnee established a village in 1746 where Shawneetown, Illinois, is today. The Illinois warred against the Shawnee and forced them to abandon the town by 1748, and continued fighting occurred between them from 1748 to 1751. By 1748, the once mighty Illinois confederation could still field warriors to defend themselves, but their total population had dwindled to between 3000-3500 members. In 1755, Illinois Indians attacked and drove away some Kickapoo and Miami who had attempted to settle on the Iroquois River. In addition, the Sauk and Fox continued raids against the Illinois in the early 1760s, when they and other tribes invaded and controlled Northern Illinois. In the mid-1750s through the mid-1760s, the Illinois would be pulled into the French war with the British and Pontiac's Rebellion, or so-called Conspiracy. These conflicts would hasten their decline.

Chapter Four

The French and Indian War and Pontiac

Frenchmen began establishing permanent settlements in Illinois in 1699, beginning with Cahokia. The French further expanded their presence with additional settlements: Kaskaskia in 1711, St. Phillippe in 1719, and Prairie du Rocher in 1722. The French ruled the area encompassing Illinois from Canada until 1717, when King Louis XV ordered the French Province of Louisiana to annex the Illinois country. Sent from Louisiana, Lieutenant Pierre Broisbriant, with one hundred soldiers, established a government for Illinois at Kaskaskia in 1718. Broisbriant began building Fort des Chartres (hereafter referred to as Fort Chartres) four miles west of the current town of Prairie du Rocher in 1718 and completed it in 1720. The French built palisades of squared logs with earth in between and bastions built diagonally from opposite corners. They also contracted several buildings: barracks for the soldiers, powder magazines, a storehouse, and the commander's home.

Beginning from this period, the French, with a growing population and a military presence at Fort Chartres, would maintain a high degree of influence over the Illinois Indians, but their rule over the remainder of the state not directly occupied was very limited until 1765 when the British took over control from them. In these years, the French used the Illinois Indians to defend their own interests. They persuaded the Illinois to join them in expeditions against the Natchez in 1729 and the Chickasaw in 1736 and 1739 in what is now the state of Mississippi. For example, in the 1736 expedition under orders from

Governor Le Moyne de Bienville, Major Pierre Artaguett, with thirty soldiers, one hundred volunteers, and two hundred Indians, marched out to join him in a military expedition against the hostile Chickasaws. Artaguette met Chevalier Vincennes from the fort of the same name with reinforcements of twenty men and another one hundred and six Indians. Together, without waiting for Bienville, they ventured an attack against the Chickasaw's stronghold. The Chickasaws ambushed and defeated the French and their allies and captured D' Artaguette, Vincennes, many other officers, and about sixteen soldiers. Failing to receive a ransom for them, the Chickasaws then proceeded to roast them at the stake, taking an entire day to complete the process.

Just before the beginning of the French and Indian War, the French were preparing to defend their empire claims in Illinois and the entire Mississippi and Ohio Valley region. Thus, construction began on a second Fort Chartres in 1753 after the Mississippi River had destroyed the first one. French workmen built limestone walls fifteen feet high and over two feet thick with forty-eight loopholes at regular intervals and two portholes for cannon in the face and two in the flank of each bastion. There was a fifteen-foot-high arched gateway with a stone platform above the gate. The fort contained a powder magazine, a storehouse two stories high, a prison with four dungeons, barracks and quarters for officers, bake ovens, a chapel and missionary quarter, and two large wells. When completed, the thirty-foot by ninety-foot fortification ranked the best the French had built in the Mississippi Valley. Enclosing four acres, it was large enough to hold four hundred soldiers when completed in 1755.

During the French and Indian War, the French recruited the Illinois Indians in their war for empire against the British. In particular, the French recruited the Peorias, considered the most warlike and more robust than the rest of the combined Illinois tribes in the Confederacy. Captain

Louis Coulon de Villers departed Fort Chartres in 1754 to assist in removing the British force under George Washington from building a fort at the forks of the Ohio (modern-day Pittsburgh). Washington, who had killed ten Frenchmen, including Louis" brother, Ensign Coulon de Villiers de Jumonville, the previous year, built Fort Necessity at Great Meadows when he learned of the French approach.

Unfortunately, the young, inexperienced twenty-two-year-old Washington had chosen disadvantageous low ground for the fort's location. On July 3, about eight hundred French and Indians commanded by de Villiers poured down deadly fire on the fort from the protected, surrounding, and forested high ground. After a brief four-hour battle, heavy rain flooded Washington's position and wetted the gunpowder. The next day (July 4), Washington surrendered his four hundred men in Fort Necessity in what would be the only time in his future illustrious career.

De Villers also captured Fort Granville in Pennsylvania with the assistance of the Illinois Indians. In 1755, Captain Nevon de Villiers led a convoy of one hundred twenty tons of flour and forty tons of salted pork up the Ohio River for the troops at Fort Duquesne. Also, in 1755, three Illinois Indians traveled east to assist the French in fighting the British. One Illinois chief fought against English settlers in Virginia. Some Illinois even raised as far as Georgia and Carolina in service of the French.

In 1757, the Illinois commandant Macarty-Mactigue, stationed at Fort Chartres, ordered Captain Charles Phillippe Aubry to travel up the Ohio River to the mouth of the Tennessee River. With his force of one hundred and ten Frenchmen, one hundred Indians, and three artillery pieces, Aubry was to reconnoiter the Tennessee in search of a rumored Anglo-Indian attack and to establish a retrenchment to hold fifty men. Aubry then decided to build Fort Massac (first named "Fort de L

Ascension") on a bluff northwest of the mouth of the Tennessee River near modern Metropolis, Illinois. That same year, Fort Massac's garrison repulsed a major Cherokee attack. Indians killed a total of fifteen men and two officers near the fort between 1758 and 1769.

Other contingents from Fort Chartres played essential roles during the war. In 1758, Charles Philippe Aubry departed for Fort Duquesne (at modern Pittsburgh) with seventeen bateaux carrying troops and supplies. While there in September, he led the Illinois contingent in routing a British force of eight hundred forty men under Major James Grant, capturing Grant in the process. Later, they abandoned the fort in the face of General John Forbes' advancing army and retreated to Illinois.

In 1759, Aubry again departed from Fort Chartres with a combined force of four hundred French and Indians from Fort Chartres up the Ohio and to Fort Niagara. This time, he met with disaster after joining a force under Captain de Ligneris to relieve the siege of the fort by Sir William Johnson's army. A British and Iroquois force of 1200 attacked and routed the French and captured Aubry. The Illinois contingent lost six officers, thirty- two soldiers, fifty-four militiamen, and several Illinois warriors in the defeat.

Illinois was not included in the French-Canadian surrender to the British in 1760 at Montreal. The French in Illinois continued their occupation as they believed the war was ongoing and prepared for an expected British attack. The attack never materialized, partly because in 1763, the Ottawa war chief Pontiac, who resided near Detroit, began a rebellion against the British who had occupied the French forts in the Great Lakes region. Pontiac and his allies had quickly become disillusioned with the British since they had refused to supply them with ammunition for hunting. They also priced trade goods higher than the Indians expected, did not distribute presents like the French, and prohibited the sale of rum. In addition, the French in

Illinois were encouraging the Indians to continue their fighting against the British. They falsely told them that the French king would be sending reinforcements. According to the Shawnees, the French sent a war belt to the Weas.

During Pontiac's Rebellion, Illinois was cut off from the British, and the French continued to occupy Illinois. Initially, Pontiac and his allies succeeded against the British, capturing nine of eleven forts west of the Appalachian Mountains. The Indians failed to take forts Detroit and Pitt and were defeated by Colonel Henry Bouquet at the Battle of Bushy Run in August 1763. Pontiac's allies sought peace when they learned the French signed the Treaty of Paris in February 1763. In addition, British/Colonial expeditions were advancing into their territory. They then ceded the land west of the Appalachians to the British.

Pontiac fled to Illinois in 1764, seeking new allies to continue the war against the British. While there, he sent out a war belt inviting other Indian nations to continue fighting against the English. He did this partly because some French residents supposedly apprised him to help a new French army sent by the King of France in the spring of 1766. If the Indians could keep the British out of Illinois until then, they could retain their lands. Pontiac and his representatives attempted to persuade Commandant Neyon de Villiers at Fort Chartres to aid them against the British, but de Villers withheld any aid de Villers later stated that if the British had informed him of peace between Britain and France, he could have prevented the Indian uprising.

Pontiac had also received a promise from the Illinois Indians that they would cooperate with him. Other than helping to prevent the British from traveling to Fort Chartres nine times between 1763 and 1765, offensive aid had yet to materialize. However, the Illinois Indians did inform British representative John Ross, who arrived at Fort Chartres in February 1763, that they did not want to see the British in Illinois. Pontiac had yet to learn that the

Shawnee had made peace or that a peace treaty between the French and British had been concluded.

Meanwhile, George Croghan had been ordered by William Johnson and General Gage to travel to Illinois and inform the French that the British would soon be coming to occupy the region. In April, Croghan's assistant, Lieutenant Alexander Fraser, arrived at Fort des Chartres to inform the St. Ange, the fort's commander, and the Indians gathered there. Though Pontiac himself was finally convinced that the peace treaty was genuine and that further resistance was futile, not all Indians were convinced. Unfortunately, a Shawnee chief, Charlot Kaske, on his return from a trip to New Orleans to see the Governor, came on a boat loaded with ammunition. He then lied to the gathered Indians, telling them that the French King was going to declare war on England within a month and that he had sent the French traders with the ammunition. In addition, Croghan was delayed from leaving an Indian congress at Fort Pitt and had not shown up at Fort Chartres as scheduled. The resident French further incited the Indians to continue hostilities by spreading the lie that the British wanted to remove the Illinois Confederation so they could settle their enemies, the Cherokee, in Illinois. An unfortunate event would soon lead to an end to the threat of continued Indian war emanating from Illinois.

Still hostile, Kickapoos from Illinois intercepted George Croghan and a party of Shawnee sent by to negotiate with Pontiac. The Kickapoos attacked Croghan's party of fifteen near the mouth of the Wabash (at present-day Shawneetown, Illinois). They killed two whites three accompanying Shawnee, and wounded everyone else, including Croghan, who was wounded in the thigh and tomahawked in the head. The Kickapoos quickly learned that they had killed Shawnee Indians. Frenchmen had told them that the Indians traveling with Croghan were Cherokee. They then took Croghan to Vincennes. In fear of the retribution of other Indians for their murder of the Shawnee accompanying Croghan and the chastisement of visiting Kickapoo and Mascouten chiefs from Illinois, they released Croghan. Soon, Croghan met Pontiac, who finally realized the hopelessness of further resistance to the British with French support. A final peace treaty was signed in late summer at a Detroit conference.

In the Fall of 1765, Captain Thomas Stirling arrived in Illinois with a detachment of one hundred men to take possession of the British. Finding Fort Massac destroyed, having been burned to the ground by the Chickasaws, he moved on to Fort Chartres in October to take command from St. Ange de Bellerive. Many of the Illinois Indians fled after the British arrival. It has been estimated that at the time of the British arrival in Illinois, only six hundred warriors remained in the Confederacy.

Starved Rock Legend

In the aftermath of Pontiac's Rebellion and the early years of British rule in Illinois, one event has given birth to a famous legend. That event was the assassination of Pontiac, which led to the subsequent destruction of the Illinois Indians at Starved Rock.

In one account, Pontiac fled to Illinois to a location on the Kankakee River with about two hundred of his warriors. Kineboo, the Illinois head chief, told Pontiac that his band was on Illinois land and gave them two moons to leave. However, Kineboo backed down from settling the issue by force when he discovered that the Potawatomi would aid Pontiac in any dispute. In one account told by Chief Shick Shack to Nehemiah Matson, a party of about thirty Ottawa hunters, including Pontiac, were on a Buffalo hunt west of Starved Rock. A large party of Illinois warriors attacked and killed most of them, but a wounded Pontiac escaped. A brutal and bloody war ensued between the Ottawa and Potawatomi against the Illinois. The Illinois Indians sought peace, and a council met at the present site of Joliet. During a speech in which Pontiac argued that peace would not be made unless his terms were accepted, Kineboo drew a knife and stabbed him in the heart.

In another account, at a council in 1766, Pontiac stabbed the Illinois chief, Black Dog. Then, in 1769, a nephew of Black Dog assassinated Pontiac, possibly as revenge for the murder of Black Dog in Cahokia. Whatever the true account of Pontiac's death, according to the legends, as a result of Pontiac's assassination, the Ottawa and their Potawatomi, Kickapoo, and Winnebago allies embarked on a war of extermination against the Illinois Indians. First appearing in written form in the 1830s, it was reported that a group of Illinois Indians fearing retaliation from Pontiac's allies after his death in 1769 retreated to Starved Rock, where most of them starved to death under a siege by Pontiac's allies.

As the story goes, after Pontiac's death, all the Illinois villages along the Illinois River were attacked and destroyed by the Allies. The exception was the well-fortified town of La Vantum, inhabited by 10,000 remaining Illinois Indians, of whom 2000 were warriors. Toward the end of the summer, during a great feast, the inhabitants suddenly saw a large Indian army moving across the meadow toward them. In front of them, the army carried the skull and crossbones of Pontiac, showing that no quarter would be given or asked. Though some enemy scaled the breastworks and entered the town, the attack was repulsed.

The next morning, the enemy renewed the battle and was repulsed once again. After a council that night, the enemy attacked a third time. The combatants fought a bloody, day-long battle that ended with a heavy rainstorm. That night, the remnant of about 1200 Illinois Indians retreated across the river and secured themselves into a supposedly safe position on top of Starved Rock. What happened next is the basis for the legend.

The following is Matson's narrative of the event, slightly abbreviated. It is perhaps the most detailed and dramatic description of the siege.

> The allied forces forded the river on the rapids, surrounded Starved Rock, and prepared themselves for ascending it in order to complete their victory. With deafening yells the warriors crowded up the rocky pathway, but on reaching the summit they were met by brave Illinoisans, who, with war-clubs and tomahawks, sent them bleeding and lifeless down the rugged precipice. Others ascended the rock to take part in the fight, but they, too, met the fate of their comrades. Again and again the assailants rallied, and rushed forward to assist their friends, but one after another were slain on reaching its summit, and their lifeless bodies thrown from the rock into the river. On came fresh bands of assents, who were made valiant by their late victory, and the fearful struggle continued until the rock was red and slippery with human gore. After losing many of their bravest warriors, the attacking forces abandoned the assault and retired from the bloody scene...
>
> On a high, rocky cliff south of Starved Rock, and known as Devil's Nose, the allied forces erected a temporary fortification. During the night they collected small timbers and evergreen brush, with which they erected a breastwork. From this breastwork they fired on the besieged, killing some and wounding others, among the latter was Kineboo, the head chief of the tribe. The fortifications protecting the south part of Starved Rock, had fallen into decay, forty-one years having elapsed since the French abandoned Fort St. Louis.

The palisades had rotted off, and the earthworks moldered away to one-half their original height, consequently they afforded but little protection. To remedy the defect on this side of the old fortress, the besieged cut down some of the stunted cedars that crowded the summit of the rock, with which they erected barricades along the embankment to shield themselves from the arrows and rifle balls of the enemy.

The besieged were now protected from the missiles of their assailants, but another enemy equally dreaded-that of hunger and thirst-began to alarm them. When they took refuge here on the rock, they carried with them a quantity of provisions, but this supply was now exhausted and starvation stared them in the face. At first this rock was thought to be a haven of safety, but now it was likely to be their tomb, and without a murmur brave warriors made preparations to meet their fate. Day after day passed away, mornings and evenings came and went, and still the Illinoisans continued to be closely guarded by the enemy, leaving them no opportunity to escape from their rocky prison.

Famishing with thirst caused them to cut up some of their buckskin clothing, out of which they made cords to draw water out of the river, but the besiegers had placed a guard at the base of the rock, and as soon as the vessel reached the water they would cut the cord, or by giving it a quick jerk the water drawer would be drawn over the precipice, and his body fall lifeless into the river...

They had been twelve days on the rock, closely guarded by the enemy, much of the time suffering from hunger and thirst. Their small stock of provision was long since exhausted, and early and late the little ones were heard crying for food...

One of the squaws, the wife of a noted chief,

while suffering in a fit of delirium caused by hunger and thirst, threw her infant from the summit of the rock into the river below, and with a wild, piercing scream, followed it.

A few brave warriors attempted to escape their prison, but on descending from the rock were slain by the vigilant guards. Others in their wild frenzy hurled their tomahawks at the fiends below, and singing their death song, laid down to die.

Proud young warriors preferred to die upon this strange rocky fortress by starvation and thirst, rather than surrender themselves to the scalping knives of a victorious enemy. Many had died; their remains were lying here and there on the rock, and the effluvium caused by putrefaction greatly annoyed the besiegers.

A party of the allied forces now ascended the rock and tomahawked all those who had survived the famine. They scalped old and young, and left the remains to decay on the rock, where their bones were seen many years afterward.

According to Matson, the Illinois Indians were exterminated here save one partly white (French Indian) who escaped towards the end of the siege during a storm by letting himself down into the river by an attached cord. He later converted to Christianity and went by the name Charles La Bell. His descendants settled near Prairie du Rocher, and one participated in a suit to recover land where the city of Peoria now stands. In his notes, Matson names several old Indians he had spoken with who stated that their fathers were at the siege of Starved Rock on the side of the besieging Indians. These accounts conflicted, so Matson cautioned the reader to draw his conclusions. For example, one Indian said only one person escaped the siege, while another said seven escaped.

An Evaluation of the Legend

Mark Walczynski makes the case in his book *Massacre 1769: The Search for the Origin of the Legend of Starved Rock* that no recorded official historical documents provided evidence that the event ever happened. He states that the Illinois Indians had last occupied the area near Starved Rock in 1752. Walczynski contradicts the assertion by Matson and others that the Illinois ceased to exist after being massacred on Starved Rock by arguing that there was an abundance of evidence of the existence of the Illinois Indians after Pontiac's death even though there was an expectation of revenge by Pontiac's allies. For example, Lieutenant Colonel John Wilkins, the commander of Fort de Chartres, reported that the Illinois Indians stayed near the vicinity of the fort through the year 1772. Wilkins gave the Indians powder and lead, but the only report of violence was the scalping of six Kaskaskias. Walczynski notes that two bands of Illinois joined with George Rogers Clark in 1778 and mentions several land sales the Illinois made by treaty. In 1773, the Illinois sold land to a British company; in 1803, the Kaskaskia ceded most of their land in Illinois at the Treaty of Vincennes; in 1818, the Peoria signed the Treaty of Edwardsville, and finally, in 1832, the Illinois Indians relinquished the remainder of their lands in Missouri and Illinois to the U. S. government. Today, the Peoria Indians live in Oklahoma.

Walczyinski mentions that in 1821, Henry Schoolcraft found no evidence of remaining bones or discarded weapons. According to the Starved Rock legend, as many as 2000 Illinois were under siege; Walczyinski argues that this is extremely unlikely as the area on top of the rock is only about one-half of an acre. In addition, he cites the absence of any archaeological evidence, mentioning the results of several digs on the summit, stating, "The summit of Starved Rock is devoid of any physical evidence, e.g., gun parts, skeletal remains, or other war material, that substantiates the accounts of the destruction of the Illinois Indians in 1769 or any other time. He concludes that the legend of Starved Rock, the name of which did not appear until 1834, is derived from the previously mentioned 1722 siege by the Fox. Let the reader decide which is the correct interpretation of the event.

Summary of Part I Colonial Period

The control of Illinois by the Illinois Confederation was never seriously threatened by the Iroquois after the 1684 attack on La Vantum. After that year, the Iroquois only made minor raids into Illinois. The Iroquois turned their attention to the French in 1687. That year, the Marquis de Denonville invaded and devastated the Seneca homeland with 3000 men. Until King William's War ended in 1697, the Iroquois allied with the British and fought against the French.

The Illinois fought alongside the French during the Fox Wars. From the defeat of the Fox until the French defeat in the French and Indian War, the Illinois were steadily weakened by almost continuous warfare. During this period, they fought against nearly every neighboring tribe in the region, including the Sioux, Osage, Shawnee, Kickapoo, Sauk, Fox, Potawatomi, Ottawa, Chippewa, Chickasaw, and others. In addition, the French recruited them to fight in expeditions against the Chickasaw and the British. They no longer exerted any control over large portions of Illinois. Sauk, Fox, Potawatomi, Kickapoo, and others had intruded onto their former territory. The Sauk and Fox began moving into and establishing control in Northern Illinois in 1764. Different tribes controlled various regions in Illinois.

Before the American Revolution, some Kaskaskia

moved to the Arkansas River, and some Peoria moved to the St. Louis area, although some of both tribes moved back in 1777. By the time of the American Revolution, when George Rogers Clark led his expedition into Illinois, the number of Illinois Indians was significantly reduced, and they could only muster one hundred to three hundred warriors.

While the French exerted considerable influence over the Illinois Indians, their small numbers prevented them from controlling the large portion of the state they did not occupy. In 1723, there were only about three hundred and thirty-four Frenchmen in Illinois, four hundred-six hundred in 1732, 2000 by 1752, and six hundred by 1769. In the years after the defeat of the Fox tribe, the various tribes no longer needed protection from the French and began to regard them as intruders. Some tribes even started to trade with the British and attacked individuals and small parties of Frenchmen.

The British presence in Illinois, starting with their occupation of Fort Chartres in 1765, resulted in very little actual governance of the territory. In 1766, George Croghan made peace with twenty-two bands or tribes in the region. For the most part, peace with the Indians reigned, only marred by the waylaying and killing of several Englishmen on the Ohio River by the Kickapoo and a few killings near Kaskaskia after Pontiac's assassination. Due to the hostility of Pontiac's allies, some Illinois Indians moved to the Arkansas River.

The British ruled the Illinois French settlements from Fort Chartres and Kaskaskia. A few American traders entered the territory and caused trouble with the small resident French population, many of whom abandoned their homes and moved west across the Mississippi River. British/Colonial trade did not flourish as the Indians remained passively hostile, and the natural trade flow was with New Orleans. No permanent civil government was ever really set up in the territory. General Gage administered the territory from New York. He wanted to abandon the territory to save on expenses, and British Ministers wished to keep the area as a preserve for the Indians. Partially to deter Americans from settling in the area, the Quebec Act of 1774 transferred the government of Illinois to Canada. The Act relieved the French from the rule of any American colonial subjects and allowed the French inhabitants to exercise their religion freely.

Part II
The Revolutionary War

Chapter Five

George Rogers Clark

Kaskaskia had become the center of British power after the British abandoned Fort Chartres in the winter of 1771-1772, fearing that the Mississippi River would soon undermine the river-facing wall in spring flooding (which it did the following year). The river had been two hundred and fifty feet from the fort walls in 1765. By 1771, the river had moved to within thirty feet of the fort. Captain Lord Hugh took two companies and occupied Fort Gage in Kaskaskia. Though Kaskaskia and Illinois were far removed from the main theater of the Revolutionary War, it would be the location of one of the only two significant battles fought in Illinois. It may even be called a non-battle because the capture of Kaskaskia was bloodless. Twenty-five-year-old George Rogers Clark and his men captured Kaskaskia in July of 1778. Clark's capture of Kaskaskia and subsequent campaigns would culminate in an American conquest of Illinois. The reasons for Clark's campaign in Illinois originated in Kentucky.

Since the beginning of the settlements in Kentucky in 1775, the inhabitants suffered constantly from the danger of Indian attacks. Even Clark was cooped up in Harrodsburg during a siege by Shawnees under Chief Blackfish. Clark had come to Kentucky in 1775 to survey for an Ohio land company. In 1776, he tried to get himself elected as a representative of Kentucky, which was not yet part of Virginia, and traveled to Virginia to obtain gunpowder (he received five hundred pounds of desperately needed powder).

Back in Kentucky in 1777, Clark concluded that to deter the Indians from attacking the Kentucky settlements, the Americans needed to go on the offensive and take the fighting to Indian Territory. The year was named the bloody 7s due to all the Indian attacks. These attacks were instigated by Lieutenant Governor of Canada Henry Hamilton, who let loose fifteen bands of Indians in the region. The Indians, mostly Shawnee, attacked both Harrodsburg and Boonesborough three times. Mc Clelland's Station had been abandoned at the beginning of the year due to Indian attacks, and Logan's Fort had also been attacked. In between assaults, settlers outside the forts were killed by Indians constantly lurking in the vicinity. Clark concluded that the only way to halt the dangerous Indian threat and protect the approximately two hundred and fifty Kentucky settlers was to strike the areas where the British were organizing and supplying the Indians.

The two centers of British power in the region were Detroit and the French settlements in Illinois, Kaskaskia being the largest with about five hundred inhabitants. Clark decided that Kaskaskia should be a prime target. From Kaskaskia, the Americans could secure their supply line from New Orleans, reduce supplies sent to Detroit, control the Indians, and eventually use it as a base to attack Detroit. Clark then sent Ben Linn and Sam Moore to spy on Kaskaskia. They reported that the British troops had vacated Kaskaskia and that the fort was in poor condition. Clark also learned that Raimond du Rastel de Rocheblave had been appointed Lieutenant Governor by the British and was in command there. Rocheblave, who had orders to inform the Indians that they would be greatly rewarded for American scalps, was probably supplying the Indians from there. However, some people were sympathetic to the American cause.

Despite his youth, Clark came from a strongly militaristic family. Five of the six Clark brothers were officers in the American Revolution and had learned the essentials of military craft. Supposedly, Clark received instruction from George Muse, who was also thought to have taught tactics to George Washington. Clark partook in a raid on a Shawnee town in 1774 and served under Andrew Lewis at the Battle of Point Pleasant in Dunmore's War. After entering Kentucky, he helped defend McClelland's station from an Indian attack.

With a plan to attack Kaskaskia, Clark again traveled to Virginia to obtain permission and funds from Virginia Governor Patrick Henry to raise a militia. Clark received permission, promotion to lieutenant colonel, and a promise in writing from Thomas Jefferson, George Mason, and George Wythe, though unofficial, that they would use all their influence to ensure that all the volunteers for his expedition would receive generous land grants. Though Clark did not obtain the three hundred men that he hoped for, he left his base at the Falls of the Ohio (present Louisville, Kentucky) on June 24, 1778, with four companies of men captained by John Montgomery, Joseph Bowman, Leonard Helm, and William Harrod, a total of one hundred and seventy-five men. One company of men deserted before they left when they learned the true objective of the expedition for the first time. Clark pursued the deserters and rounded up seven or eight of them.

Clark's small army traveled down the Ohio River and stopped on an island at the mouth of the Tennessee River. On the island, Clark met a small party of hunters who had recently come from Kaskaskia. Although Clark had sent spies there the previous year, he had no current information. The hunters informed him that the British Governor Edward Abbott had recently left Vincennes to go to Detroit. The hunters also informed Clark that the militia would put up a fight if they had a warning of his coming, as they had been told that the Americans were horrible savages. The hunting party volunteered to join Clark's expedition and guided them there after landing a little below Fort Massac (near modern Metropolis Illinois). Clark's force landed there, about one hundred miles from Kaskaskia, to avoid likely detection by the French if they entered the Mississippi River. From the point below Fort Massac, Clark's small army hacked their way through the wilderness to Kaskaskia. Part of the way, they followed an old French military road with trees painted red and marked with cut-in numbers. Despite their guide losing his way, they arrived opposite Kaskaskia after six days, subsisting partly on a diet of berries. During the trip down the river, William Linn caught up with Clark after his stop at the mouth of the Tennessee River and handed him a dispatch with all-important information, such as that the French had signed an alliance with the United States.

Indeed, the expedition had been kept a secret. Later, a letter from Rocheblave to his superiors revealed that he had a report of a force going down the Ohio River, but he believed it was headed for New Madrid. Although he had kept the people armed just a few days before Clark's arrival, he relaxed his guard just before Clark's attack. The attack was so surprising that even two months after Clark's capture of Kaskaskia, Henry Hamilton, the British lieutenant governor at Detroit, did not know who was responsible.

Kaskaskia and Cahokia

The following is Clark's account (Edited by Milo M. Quaife) of the actual conquest of Kaskaskia, Cahokia, and the surrounding villages and the taking of Vincennes written down perhaps ten years after the events occurred.

On the evening of July fourth we arrived within a few miles of the town, where we threw out scouts in advance and lay until nearly dark. We then resumed our march and took possession of a house on the bank of the Kaskaskia River, about three-quarters of a mile above the town, occupied by a large family. We learned from the inmates that the people had been under arms a few days before but had concluded the alarm to be groundless and at present all was quiet, and that there was a large number of men in town, although the Indians were for the most part absent. We obtained from the man boats enough to convey us across the river, where I formed my force in three divisions. I felt confident the inhabitants could not now obtain knowledge of our approach in time to enable them to make any resistance. My object was now to get possession of the place with as little confusion as possible, but to have it if necessary at the loss of the whole town. I did not entirely credit the information given us at the house, as the man seemed to contradict himself, informing us among other things that noise we heard in the town was caused by the negroes at a dance. I set out for the fort with one division, ordering the other two to proceed to different quarters of the town. If I met with no resistance, at a certain signal a general shout was given and a certain part of the town was to be seized immediately, while men from each detachment who were able to talk French were to run through the streets proclaiming what had happened and informing the townsmen to remain in their houses on pain of being shot down.

These arrangements produced the desired effect, and within a very short time we were in complete possession of the place, with every avenue guarded to prevent any one from escaping and giving the alarm to the other villages. Various orders not worth mentioning had been issued for the guidance of the men in the event of opposition. Greater silence, I suppose, never regained among the inhabitants of a town than in Kaskaskia at this juncture; not a person was to be seen or a word to be heard from them for some time. Meanwhile our troops purposely kept up the greatest possible noise throughout every quarter of the town, while patrols moved around it continually throughout the night, as it was a capital object to intercept a message that might be sent out. In about two hours all the inhabitants were disarmed, and informed that anyone who should be taken while attempting to escape from the place would immediately be put to death. Mr. Rocheblave was secured, but some time elapsed before he could be gotten out of his room. I suppose he delayed to tell his wife what disposition to make of his public papers, but few of which were secured by us. Since his chamber was not entered during the night, she had ample opportunity to dispose of them, but how she did it we could never learn. I do not suppose she put them in her trunks, although we never examined them. From the idea she entertained of us she must have expected the loss even of her clothes.

During the night I sent for several individuals, from whom I sought to procure information, but obtained very little that was not already known to us. We learned, however, that the conduct of several of the inhabitants indicated them to be inclined to the American cause; that a large number of Indians were in the neighborhood of Cahokia; sixty miles distant; that Mr. Cerre' a leading merchant and one of our most inveterate enemies, had left Kaskaskia with a large quantity of furs a few days before, enroute to Michilimackinac and thence to Quebec, from which place he had lately arrived at Kaskaskia; and that he was then in St. Louis, the Spanish capital, together with a considerable quantity of goods which would be useful to our men.

In addition to Cerre' information was given me about numerous other individuals. I at once suspected that the object of the informers was to make their peace with me at the expense of their neighbors, and my situation demanded of me too much caution to permit giving them much satisfaction. I found Cerre' to be one of the most eminent men in the country, with great influence over the people. I had some suspicion that his accusers were probably in debt to him and hence desired to ruin him. What I had heard led me to feel that he was an object of importance to me, since he might be wavering in his opinion respecting the merits of the war; and if he should take a decisive stand in our favor, he might prove a valuable acquisition. In short, his enemies led me to desire much to see him, and as he was then out of my power I had no doubt I could bring this about by means of his family who were in my hands. I immediately caused a guard to be stationed at his house and his stores to be sealed along with all the others. I did not doubt that when he should hear of this he would be extremely anxious for an interview.

By the morning of the fifth Messrs. Richard Winston and Daniel Murray, who proved to have attached to the American cause, had plenty of provisions prepared. After the troops had regaled themselves they were withdrawn from the town and posted in extended position on its border. Every man had been expressly forbidden to hold any conversation with the inhabitants. All was distrust; their town was in complete possession of an enemy of whom they entertained the most horrid conception, and they were unable as yet to have any conversation with one of our people. Even those I talked with were ordered to speak to any of my men. After some time they were told they could walk freely about the town. Finding they were busily engaged in conversation, I had a few of the principal militia officers put in irons, without hinting any reason or hearing anything they had to say in their own defense. The worst was now anticipated by all. I perceived the state of consternation the inhabitants were in, and in imagination, I suppose, felt all that they were experiencing in reality; and I felt perfectly disposed to act as arbiter between them and my duty.

After some time the priest obtained permission to call on me, and came accompanied by five or six elderly gentlemen. However great the shock they had already sustained by reason of their situation, the addition when they entered the room where I was sitting with my officers was obvious and great. Having left our extra clothing at the Ohio River, we were almost naked; torn by the bushes and briers, we presented a dirty and savage aspect. So shocked were they that some time elapsed before they ventured to seat themselves, and still more before they would speak. At length we asked them what they wanted. The priest stated (after inquiring which of us was the commander) that as the townsmen expected to be separated, never, perhaps, to meet again, they had commissioned him to petition for permission to spend some time in the church taking their leave of each other. I knew that they supposed their religion to be obnoxious to us. I carelessly told him, therefore, that I had nothing to say about his church and he might go there if he pleased; if he did, he was to tell the people not to leave town. They attempted to introduce some other conversation, but were told that we were not at leisure; and, after answering a few questions, which he asked with a view to discouraging them from again coming to me with petitions, as they had not yet come to the state of mind I wanted, they went away. The whole populace now seemed to assemble in the church. The infants were carried along, and the houses were left for the most part without a person in them, with the exception of a few who cared little how things went and a few more who were not so much alarmed as the majority. I issued an order prohibiting the soldiers from entering the houses.

The people remained some time in the church, and on breaking up, the priest and many of the principal citizens came to thank me for the indulgence shown them, and to be permission to address me further on a subject dearer to them than all things else. They stated that their present situation was the fate of war and they were reconciled to the loss of their property; but they hoped I would not part them from their families, and that the women and children might keep some of their clothes and a small quantity of provisions, that they might support themselves by their industry. Their entire conduct had been influenced bid their commandants, whom they felt obliged to obey, and they were not much acquainted with the American war, as they had had but little opportunity to inform themselves. Many of them, however, had expressed themselves as strongly in favor of the Americans as they had dared. In short, they said everything that sensible men in their situation could be expected to advance, and their sole hope seemed to be to secure some lenity for their women and families, supposing their property would appease us. I felt convinced there was no finesse in all this, but that they really expressed their sentiments and the height of their expectations.

    This was the point to which I had wished to bring them. I now asked them very abruptly whether they thought they were addressing savages. I told them that from the tenor of their conversation I was sure they did. Did they suppose we meant to strip the women and children or take the bread out of their mouths? Or that we would condescend to make war on women and children or the church: I informed them it was to prevent the effusion of innocent blood by the Indians, instigated thereto by their commandants and enemies, and not the prospect of plunder, that had caused thus to visit them. As soon as this object was attained we would be perfectly satisfied; and as the king of France had joined the Americans (this information affected them very visibly) it was probable the war would shortly come to an end. They were at liberty to take whichever side they pleased without danger of losing their property or having their families distressed. As for their church. all religions would be tolerated in America, and so far were we from meddling with it, that any one who offered insult to it would be punished by me. To convince them we were not savages and plunderers, as they had conceived us to be, they might return to their families and tell them to conduct themselves as usual, with entire freedom and without any apprehension of danger. I told them the information I had received since my arrival so fully convinced me that they had been influenced by false information given them by their leaders I was willing to forget all that had passed. Their friends who were in confinement would be released immediately and the guards withdrawn from every part of the town except the house of Cerre', and I only required compliance with a proclamation which I should immediately issue.

Such was the substance of my reply to them. They attempted to soften my idea that they had supposed us to be a set of savages and plunderers, or that they had supposed the property in a town belonged to those who captured it. I told them I knew they had been taught to believe that we were but little better than barbarians, but that we would say no more on the subject, and that I wished them to go and relieve the anxiety of the townsmen. Their feelings may more easily be imagined than expressed. They retired and in a few minutes the scene changed from an extreme state of dejection to one of great joy. Bells were rung, the church was crowded with people returning thanks, in short, every appearance of extravagant joy was manifested.

I immediately set about preparing a proclamation to be presented to them before they should leave the church, but wishing to test the people further, I postponed it for a few days. Feeling confident that any report that might now be sent out to the surrounding country would be favorable to us, I became more careless about who should go from or come into the town; but knowing what might yet take place, I was uneasy over

Cahokia and was determined as soon as possible to make a lodgment there and gain the place by some such stratagem as I had already employed at Kaskaskia.

I ordered Major Bowman to mount his company and part of another on horses to be procured from the town, and taking with him a few townsmen to inform their friends of what had happened, to proceed without delay to Cahokia and if possible gain possession of the place before the following morning. I gave him no further instructions on the subject, leaving him free to exercise his own judgment He gave orders for collecting the horses, whereupon a number of gentlemen came to inform me that they were aware of the design. They pointed out that the soldiers were much fatigued, and said they hoped I would not reject their offer to execute whatever I might wish to have done at Cahokia. The people there were their friends and relatives and would, they thought, follow their example. At least, they hoped, they might be permitted to accompany the detachment.

Conceiving that it might be good policy to show them that we put confidence in them (which, in fact, I desired for obvious reasons to do), I told them I had no doubt Major Bowman would welcome their company and that as many as chose might go. Although we were too weak to be other than suspicious and much on our guard, I knew we had sufficient security for their good behavior. I told them that if they went at all they ought to go equipped for war. I was in hopes that everything would be settled amicably, but as it was the first time they had ever borne arms as freemen it might be well to equip themselves and see how they felt, especially as they were about to put their friends in the same situation as themselves.

They appeared to be highly pleased at this idea, and in the evening the Major set out with a force but little inferior to the one with which we had entered the country, the Frenchmen being commanded by their former militia officers. These new friends of ours were so elated over the thought of the parade they were to make at Cahokia that they were too much concerned about equipping themselves to appear to the best advantage. It was night before the party moved and the distance being twenty leagues, it was night before the party moved and the distance being twenty leagues, it was late in the morning of the sixth before they reached Cahokia. Detaining every person they met, they entered the outskirts of the town before they were discovered. The townsmen were at first much alarmed by this sudden appearance of strangers in hostile array and being ordered even by their friends and relatives to surrender the town. As the confusion among the women and children over the cry of the Big Knives being in town proved greater than had been anticipated, the Frenchmen immediately informed the people what had happened at Kaskaskia. Major Bowman told them not to be alarmed; that although resistance was out of the question he would convince them that he would prefer their friendship to their hostility. He was authorized to inform them that they were at liberty to become free Americans as their friends at Kaskaskia had done. Any who did not care to adopt this course were free to leave the country except such as had been engaged in inciting the Indians to war.

Cries of liberty and freedom, and huzzahs for the Americans rang through the whole town. The gentlemen from Kaskaskia dispersed among their friends and in a few hours all was amicably arranged, and Major Bowman snugly quartered in the old British fort. Some individuals said the town had been given up too tamely, but little attention was paid to them. A considerable number of Indians who were encamped in the neighborhood (Cahokia was an important center of Indian trade) immediately fled. One of the townsmen who was at St. Louis, some time later wrote a letter to me excusing himself for not paying me a visit. By July 8, Major Bowman had everything settled agreeably to our wishes. All of the inhabitants cheerfully took the oath of allegiance, and he set about repairing the fort and regulating the internal police of the place.

The neighboring villages Prairie du Rocher and St. Phillippe followed the example set by Kaskaskia and Cahokia, and since we made not strict inquiry concerning those who had been engaged in encouraging the Indians to war, within a few days the country appeared to be in a state of perfect harmony. Friendly correspondence which was at once commenced between the Spanish officers and ourselves added much to the general tranquility and happiness. It was not my fortune to enjoy pleasures of this kind. I found myself embarked on an enterprise that would require close attention and all the skill of which I was master to execute that service for my country which now appeared in prospect, with honor to it and with credit to myself.

Vincennes

The day after Clark captured Kaskaskia, he sent Simon Kenton, Shadrach Bond, and Elisha Batty to scout Vincennes. Shortly after Bond returned with a report on

Vincennes and after obtaining the allegiance of the Kaskaskians and Cahokians, Clark sent the pro-American priest, Father Pierre Gibault, to Vincennes to gain the allegiance of the inhabitants, the threat that if they refused expert "all the miseries of war." On July 14, the townspeople were won over to the American side, and Captain Leonard Helm was sent to take command.

Clark and Helm quickly went to work on a diplomatic offensive with the surrounding Indians, informing them that their old Father, the French king, now wanted them to make peace with the Americans and fight along with him and the Big Knives against the British. Clark won over the local Illinois Indians, and near Vincennes, a paramount Piankeshaw chief called the "Big Door" because of his powerful influence over so many were won to the American side. Within a few months, Clark made peace with ten to twelve tribes up to Lake Michigan. The French in Illinois told the Indians how well-treated they were by the Americans and advised them to make peace with them. The Spanish in St. Louis, governed by Don Fernando Leyba, also spoke favorably of the Americans to help convince them to make peace with the Americans.

Clark had personally contacted the Spanish Governor at St. Louis, Don Fernando Leyba. Leyba, who had only taken up his position a month before Clark's arrival and feared British intentions, made every effort to assist Clark materially. In addition, in what must have been arranged beforehand, in late August, sixty men from New Orleans were on their way along with goods and ammunition to reinforce Clark. Within a short period after the conquest, Clark would say it was safe, and "we could send a single soldier through any part of the Wabash and Illinois country." Nevertheless, one attempt by hostile Winnebago Indians sent to kidnap Clark was thwarted.

Clark's position did not remain secure for long. By August 6, one loyal British subject who had been in the vicinity when Clark's little army had arrived informed Henry Hamilton at Detroit of the details of the American occupation. Known as the "Hair Buyer," Hamilton was greatly hated by frontiersmen because it was thought that he paid Indians for American scalps. Hamilton had reported in January 1778 that he had received twenty-one prisoners and one hundred and twenty-nine scalps between May and September of the same year. He would receive another seventeen prisoners and eighty-one scalps. However, though it has never been proven conclusively that the British authorities paid directly for scalps, they did provide lavish gifts to the Indians when they brought them into them. Hamilton immediately abandoned plans to attack Fort Pitt and formed an expedition first to recapture Vincennes and, subsequently, to retake the Illinois country. He departed Detroit on October 7 with a small force of eighty British regulars, about the same number of militia, and seventy Indians. Since all the French militia had deserted the American commander, Captain Helm, at the approach of Hamilton, he was left with only three remaining defenders. With overwhelming odds, Hamilton obtained the surrender of Fort Sackville on December 17, 1778.

Learning in late January to early February of Hamilton's capture of Vincennes from Francis Vigo, a captured merchant whom Hamilton had unwittingly freed, Clark decided almost immediately to retake Vincennes. He later stated, "I knew if I did not take him, he would take me." Displaying incredible leadership, courage, and determination, Clark led a force of one hundred thirty-one hundred seventy men, half French militia, in the middle of winter about one hundred eighty miles to Vincennes. (Forty of the one hundred seventy men Clark counted were probably included in the force Clark sent in a gunboat up the Wabash). Marching through snow and sometimes wading through chest-deep freezing water, the men endured much suffering and hunger in an eighteen-day ordeal. It also rained about a third of the time, and the men did not have waterproof clothes or footwear.

Clark's men arrived in Vincennes about sunset. They fired on Fort Sackville until about four o'clock in the morning, wounding a few British soldiers. The Americans then ceased fire to allow a British patrol to enter the fort. Clark desired the patrol to enter the fort rather than flee to hostile Indians who could be gathered to attack Clark. Firing on the fort resumed until nine o'clock when Clark sent in a flag of truce and demanded the fort's surrender. Hamilton rejected this demand, and the firing on both sides resumed until about noon. Hamilton then offered to surrender on honorable terms. After some back-and-forth haggling in which Clark told Hamilton that he must surrender "at discretion," which meant unconditional surrender, the negotiations were interrupted when the return of a small Indian war party was spotted.

Unaware that the fort was under attack, the war party was met outside by some of Clark's men, whom they thought were welcoming them. Clark's men suddenly opened fire after the Indians had discharged their guns in celebration of the taking of scalps and killed or wounded most of them. They took nine of them prisoner and set them down in a circle in view of the fort's gate. One man whose relatives had been killed by Indians then tomahawked four Indians in full view of the fort's garrison. Not knowing when further reinforcements with supplies would arrive and under the grim belief that Clark would kill all of his men in an assault, Hamilton surrendered late that afternoon.

Clark quickly sent Captain Helm to capture the British supply boats. Helm ascended the Maumee, confiscating six tons of supplies worth 10,000 pounds. Clark then distributed clothing and liquor to his troops. Bitterly, Clark later regretted that he did not immediately march his men to assail Detroit. After a council meeting with other leaders, Clark decided to wait for the expected reinforcements. Instead of five hundred additional men, Colonel John Montgomery only brought in one hundred and fifty. Some Delaware Indians attacked settlers, and Clark diverted his men to attack their villages. Also, three hundred additional reinforcements from Kentucky under Colonel John Bowman disregarded their orders and attacked a hostile Shawnee town. Only thirty Kentuckians eventually reached Clark; the rest returned to Kentucky to defend their homes from Indian raids. Detroit had been ripe for the taking, with the surrounding French residents turning pro-American and only a garrison of one hundred men to defend it. However, Clark could not raise even the limited manpower that would be needed; the opportunity to take Detroit was lost.

     Fortunately, Clark succeeded in keeping most of the Indians at peace for a time and reduced raids on Kentucky settlements. However, Clark knew peace with the Indians was tenuous; they were ready to switch sides if the British appeared stronger. The Illinois Indians were divided during the war. Part of the Peoria tribe joined Hamilton when he captured Vincennes, while Kaskaskia Indians served the Americans as hunters and scouts. Despite the continuation of the war, most significantly, Clark's achievements would lead to the acquisition of the Old Northwest Territory by the United States from the British at the Treaty of Paris in 1783.

     Clark was the only general in the Revolutionary War who was never defeated in battle. Unfortunately, Clark impoverished himself by frequently paying for expeditions with his own resources for his young country. Sadly, neither the United States Congress nor the state of Virginia paid Clark for his heroic and precious services until years later. Clark finally received half pay of four hundred dollars a year and a sword from the Virginia General Assembly in 1812.

Chapter Six

St. Louis and Cahokia

To protect Americans on the Ohio River, Thomas Jefferson, the present governor of Virginia, wanted a fort built. Beginning in late April-early May 1780, Clark constructed Fort Jefferson, a short distance below the mouth of the Ohio. Almost as soon as Clark had finished building the fort, he left in response to a runner Montgomery had sent from Cahokia. Montgomery had requested Clark's assistance after he learned of a combined British and Indian army advancing toward him. Hurrying to Cahokia, Clark made it a day before the attack.

In 1779, both France and Spain had declared war on Britain. Lord Germain, British secretary of the colonies, ordered Fredrick Haldimand in Canada to capture all Spanish and American posts on the Mississippi River. The British needed to prevent the Spanish from supplying the Americans; they needed to secure the fur trade north of the Ohio River and mobilize their wavering Indian allies. As a part of their overall strategy to recapture the Illinois country, Major Patrick Sinclair, commander at Fort Michilimackinac sent a force of about 1200 men, including three hundred regular troops and seven hundred and fifty to nine hundred Indians, Sauks, Fox, Chippewas, Winnebagos, Ottawas, and Sioux to attack Spanish held St. Louis on the west bank of the Mississippi and American held Cahokia on the east bank. British trader and former militia captain Emmanuel Hesse commanded the entire army. At the same time, the Chippewa Chief Matchekewis had overall command of the Indians, of which the two hundred Sioux under Wapasha were the largest contingent.

Spanish Louisiana Governor Fernando de Leyba learned ahead of time from scouts about Hesse's advance. Montgomery also knew of the British advance and consulted with Leyba about sending a combined Spanish and American force upriver to attack the British and Indians before they reached the immediate vicinity. As the Spanish would have to provide most of the transportation and supplies, they did not reach an agreement.

Leyba defended St. Louis with about three hundred men, including twenty-nine regulars. Leyba had received one hundred fifty-two well-trained French militia from Francois Valle at the site of the French Colonial Valley mines about sixty miles south of St. Louis. He built a stone tower called Fort San Carlos. The fort was thirty feet in diameter, thirty-forty feet high, and five cannons mounted on top. He also put the townspeople, of which there were about five hundred, and two hundred slaves, to work throwing up entrenchments four to five feet high around the perimeter.

Scouts that Hesse had sent to inspect the defenses around St. Louis had not been able to get because of workers in the fields around the town. Thus, the British forces were surprised by the unexpectedly strong defenses when they attacked them. This discouraged the Indians, who did not typically directly assault fortified positions. Not expecting such strong defenses, the Sauks and Fox quickly broke off the attack after the first volley or two. The Winnebagos seem to be the only ones who directly charged the defenders. They were driven rapidly back after losing a chief and three men. After the initial assault, the British and Indian forces, perhaps due to the cannon fire, took cover and kept up a fire on the entrenchments that lasted two to five hours. Leyba, sick at the time of the attack, directed the battle from the tower. The Indians tried to draw out the defenders by killing captured citizens in view of them, but Leyba prohibited any sorties. The Indians then withdrew from the town and ravaged the surrounding countryside. In the battle, the Spaniards lost twenty-nine killed and twenty-four wounded. Perhaps another thirty were lost, killed, or taken prisoner to the Indians marauding the residents outside the defensive perimeter; British and Indian losses are unknown.

The attack on Cahokia appears to have taken place on May 26, in conjunction with the attack on St. Louis, both battles beginning about one o'clock in the afternoon. Montgomery and George Rogers Clark led the one hundred fifty to two hundred defenders of Cahokia. Clark had arrived with a few men just the day before in response to Montgomery's request for help. The attack probably focused on the mission property in Cahokia, consisting of a stone church about sixty feet in length (Fort Bowman) and several other buildings and fortifications. The mission compound (fort) would have provided enough shelter for the women and children and a solid defensive position for the men. In any case, the Americans only had to defend about an eight-hundred-yard position, which included the stone house and other buildings. Little is known of the attack other than the Canadians under Jean Ducharme, and approximately three hundred Indians led by Chief Matchekewis advanced from the fields in the north. Their scouts had reported that there were no troops in Cahokia. However, the troops had been kept out of view. When the enemy approached, Clark emerged from the East gate to engage them. He fired a six-pounder and turned back inside the defensive perimeter. This was fortunate because he would have stumbled into an ambush if he had advanced another hundred and fifty yards. It appears that the attackers never attempted a direct assault. Both sides hollered out insults to each other and only fired from cover. During the engagement, the enemy killed five defenders, including one officer. The attacking force tried but failed to draw out the defenders from their fortified positions.

Additionally, it is believed that the attackers had learned that Clark was directing the defenders, further discouraging their efforts. The attackers broke off the fight after about an hour. Before leaving the area, they destroyed livestock and crops and captured a few citizens. After the battle, Colonel Montgomery led a force of about three hundred men, including Kaskaskia Indians, in pursuit of the attackers. Montgomery was unable to catch them. Instead, he attacked and burned the crops and the main village of the Sauk and Fox at Saukenauk near the Rock River.

Before the Revolutionary War ended, several other expeditions would originate from the French settlements around Cahokia and St. Louis. A French officer, Augustin Mottin de la Balme, appeared in the summer of 1780 to attack the British centers of power in the region. He sent one detachment of only seventeen men under Jean Baptiste Hamelin and managed to capture Fort St. Joseph at Niles, Michigan. However, the fort's commander, Lieutenant De Quindre, returned shortly after their departure. He quickly gathered a party of Potawatomi and pursued Hamelin. De Quindre caught up with them and killed or captured all but three of Hamelin's men near Chicago.

La Balme attempted to fulfill Clark's plan to capture Detroit. He led a force of about eighty Frenchmen first to a post at the Miami River near Fort Wayne and destroyed the Miami Indian village of Kekionga. Chief Little Turtle quickly gathered his warriors and destroyed La Balme's force, killing him and most of his men about ten miles southwest of Kekionga. Finally, in another effort to subdue the British, Captain Eugenie Pourre led a combined militia force of about sixty-five from St. Louis and Cahokia residents. He was later joined by another sixty Indians and marched across Illinois to capture Fort St. Joseph in early 1781. The Spanish captured the fort without a fight in Commander De Quindre's absence and raised the Spanish flag during their twenty-four-hour occupation. On this basis, the Spanish government would try to claim the land in the Paris Peace negotiations in 1783.

Chapter Seven

Post-American Revolution

After the Revolutionary War, the Illinois Indians remained friendly to the United States. Of the various tribes of the Illinois Confederation, only about twenty families of Kaskaskia remained in Illinois by 1796; the rest had crossed over to Missouri. The powerful Potawatomi, who had begun to move into Illinois in the second half of the eighteenth century and established villages along the Kankakee and Illinois Rivers after the Greenville treaty, would start to resent and resist American emigration into Illinois. They turned to the British for support around 1800 and began to harass incoming settlers. However, from the end of the Revolutionary War until the War of 1812, Illinois was plagued mostly by hostile Kickapoo Indians.

Though the Illinois Kickapoo had aided George Rogers Clark by scouting for him and the Wabash Kickapoo had sided with him when he captured Hamilton at Vincennes, as early as 1780, they started switching their allegiance back to the British and steadily increased in animosity toward the Americans as more and more settlers moved into their territory. The years 1783-1790 would prove to be very bloody as the Kickapoo and other tribes of the Northwest Territory killed an estimated 1500 American settlers north of the Ohio River.

Alternatively, many of the Kickapoo optioned to move into Spanish territory, especially after American expeditions burned their villages on the Wabash three times in the early 1790s. This happened when the Kickapoo aided Little Turtle's Miami Confederacy in their war to retain Indian lands north of the Ohio River. General

Anthony Wayne defeated the Miami-led Confederacy at the Battle of Fallen Timbers in August 1794. As a result of the Indian defeat, some of the Indian land north of the Ohio River was ceded to the Americans at the Treaty of Greenville in 1795. In addition, the United States obtained sixteen parcels of land, six square miles each, designated for building forts and trading posts.

Even after the Treaty of Greenville, the Kickapoo continued their spirited resistance to American incursions. For example, in the Spring of 1795, Kickapoo attacked settlers in Illinois at Riley's Mill, where they killed the owner and several Negroes. Kickapoo also killed Samuel Chew and a party of five, and in May, near Fort Massac, they murdered a white family and thirteen Negroes.

After 1800, the Spanish significantly reduced gifts, arms, rations, and bounties for scalps to the Kickapoo. Subsequently, many of them resettled in villages along the Illinois and Wabash Rivers. Friction quickly developed between the Kickapoo and white settlers. After settlers insulted some Kickapoo, including death threats to the son of a Kickapoo chief, the Kickapoo retaliated. They butchered animals, burned barns, and killed any settlers who resisted them. Also, they rebuffed any attempts by Territorial Governor William Henry Harrison to make peace. Increasingly, the Kickapoo came under the influence of the gift-giving British, who were wooing the tribes the various tribes of the Northwest Territory and provoking them against the Americans.

Beginning in 1805, the Shawnee Prophet, Tenskwatawa (The Loud Voice), formerly known as Lalawethika, started a movement of reform among the Northwestern Indians to discard white culture. He taught that the Indians needed to give up alcohol, white man's clothing, and even guns except for warfare, among other things, and return to the native practices of their ancestors. He and his brother Tecumseh combined this movement with the idea that the land belonged to all Indians and that all the tribes must unite against the Americans. No more land cessions were to be made. The Indians had been ceding land at an alarming rate, negotiating fifteen land treaties between 1803 and 1809.

Tecumseh and his brother established a center of Indian resistance in 1808 at Kithtippecanoe (Prophetstown), a former Kickapoo village site on Tippecanoe Creek, near present-day Battle Ground, Indiana. They chose this site as a symbol of resistance to the Americans as it was one of the sites acquired by the treaty at Greenville by the U.S. government for its establishments. Members of many tribes, Pottawatomi, Ottawa, Winnebago, Shawnee, Delaware, and Kickapoo, gathered there. At its peak, Prophetstown and the surrounding area probably had a population of around 6000, making it at the time the largest city in America west of the Appalachians.

The Illinois Potawatomi chief, Main Poc, was invited to establish a village there. Main Poc was acclaimed as the greatest warrior in the West and had the most significant influence of any other Indian then. About half of one band of Illinois Kickapoo under Chief Little Deer did seek peace with Americans, taking advice from Harrison, who advised them to stay at their homes. It is related that Tenskwatawa, or a delegate, also visited the Sauks and told them, "If you do not join your friends on the Wabash, the Americans will take this very village from you!" The Sauk did not rally to Tecumseh's cause at the time, and Black Hawk confessed later that he did not think that would happen.

Before 1809, through several treaties, Harrison had acquired almost all of Ohio, Eastern Michigan, Southern Indiana, and Western and Southern Illinois from the Indians. In 1809, he obtained a land cession of an additional 3,000,000 acres from pro-American Kickapoo, Delaware, Miami, Wea, and Potawatomi Indians. Potawatomi signed this 1809 treaty from the St. Joseph area in Michigan, which signed away lands they did not claim as their own, but they agreed to obtain annuities from the government.

This treaty infuriated Tecumseh and his allies, and afterward, they made travel in the territories very hazardous. Potawatomi in Illinois increased raids on and killing of whites, and attacks occurred around Kaskaskia, Shoal Creek, and Price Farms. Tecumseh would say to Indiana Territorial Governor William Henry Harrison at a conference in 1810 "that the Great Spirit has given them as common property to all the Indians, and that they could not, no should not be sold without the consent of all. That all tribes of Indians on the continent formed but one nation." Tecumseh again met with Harrison in July of 1811, stating that the Indians needed the lands ceded by the 1809 treaty and that the whites should move away.

Knowing that the British backed Indian land claims, that war was probably imminent, and that Tecumseh had left on a recruiting mission to the South, Harrison decided to move against the Indians gathered at Prophetstown, where there were many Illinois Kickapoo and Potawatomi included in Tenskwatawa's village of about seven hundred Indians. As he approached Prophetstown on November 6th at the head of an army of about 1000 men, an Indian came out with a white flag suspended on a pole. The Indian conversed with Harrison and assured him that the Indians desired peace and friendship with the United States. Chief White Horse, one of the Prophet's principal counselors, whom Harrison knew, and others agreed to prevent all hostilities before a meeting between Harrison and the Prophet the next day.

The Battle of Tippecanoe

The next day did not unfold as generally expected. According to Shabonna, a Potawatomi chief and a grand nephew of Pontiac, during the night, two white men persuaded the Prophet to attack Harrison's army camped less than a mile away from the village. From a captured Negro wagon driver named Ben, the Prophet learned that Harrison's army did not have any cannon with them and that Harrison intended to attack the next day. The Prophet ignored Tecumseh's command to avoid battle and decided to attack first. He bolstered the courage of the approximately five hundred to six hundred Indians present, telling them that victory was theirs and that the white man's bullets would not harm them. The gunpowder had already changed into sand, and the bullets to mud. He also told them that he had received assurance from the Master of Life that if they struck before the next sunrise, the darkness would hide them, and they would achieve victory.

In another version, according to the Kickapoo, two Winnebagos had been shot the night before the battle while they were on patrol. This incident prompted the Indians to seek revenge. Long after the battle, Tenskwatawa stated, "The Winnebagos with me at Tippecanoe struck your people. I was opposed but could not stop it." The Indians also never mentioned Tenskwatawa's use of magic.

The Indians, primarily Winnebago, and Kickapoo, with contingents of Shawnee, Wyandot, Potawatomi, and Piankeshaw, moved into positions around the quadrangle-shaped camp in the hours before dawn. According to various sources, Indian leadership has been attributed to Mengotowa of the Kickapoo and Waweapakoosa of the Winnebago. And Shabbona, Waubonsee, Winnamac of the Potawatomi, White Loon, and Stone Eater. The Kickapoo were to fire on one side of the camp and the Winnebago on the other. The Indian force of between four hundred to five hundred men were to creep on their bellies to get as close as possible before assaulting Harrison's army. They were attempting to sneak into camp first to kill Harrison, whom they had been observing through the march to Prophetstown and whom they had been given the opportunity to shoot many times. The Prophet had foretold the army's disintegration if they could first kill Harrison. However, shortly before 4:00 a.m., their plans were swept aside. First, two pickets, Private William Brigham and William Brown, heard an arrow swish past them, and they turned to run back to camp. Then Corporal Stephen Mars of Geiger's Kentucky Volunteers, a sharp-eyed sentry, spotted an Indian and shot him. Mars started back towards camp but was slain before he could enter the American lines. The wounded Indian cried out. Immediately, the others rose and began yelling, expecting the soldiers to run away.

The troops responded quickly to the yells, which only served to alert them to the danger. If the attack had started just four minutes later, they would already have been in their positions in a single rank around the camp perimeter-Harrison was putting on his boots and preparing to give the order to arouse the men when the attack began. Nevertheless, the Indians first hit Captain Barton's and Captain Geiger's company on the left angle of the rear line. Isaac Naylor stated that the Indians were already charging the line less than a minute after he heard the first two rifle shots. Inside the camp, the men were targets in the light of the fires that had been left burning since many did not have blankets or tents. Early in the battle, Indian sharpshooters took full advantage and inflicted casualties before the soldiers extinguished the fires.

A few Indians penetrated the lines and were quickly killed in the center of the camp. One was cut down while attempting to tomahawk Captain Geiger in the back of his tent, where he had gone to fetch a new weapon for a soldier who had lost his gun. Indians had their sights set on Harrison, who they knew rode a gray mare. Harrison had mounted a horse at the first sounds of battle. His horse had broken its tether and could not be found. Instead, Harrison had mounted a bay. His aide, Abraham Owen, had rushed out to join Harrison. After jumping on his light-colored horse, he was immediately fired on from the ambush and killed. Harrison stated afterward that he thought the Indians were trying to kill him because they had been waiting for him to mount his gray horse. Harrison survived the assassination attempt but did suffer an abrasion to his head when a bullet passed through his hat.

Harrison's first response to the attack was to ride immediately toward the rear northeast angle, which received the first Indian charge. Seeing that the Indians were severely punishing Barton's company, thirteen of his raw recruits had already fled toward the center of the camp. He quickly reinforced them with Cook's and Wentworth's companies (now under Lieutenant Peters). He then busied himself rushing to and fro from one part of the perimeter to the other, sending reinforcements where needed most. The Indians had not moved into their positions, having been forced into battle before final preparations by the firing of the sentry. Harrison later said, "My great object was to keep the lines entire, to prevent the enemy from breaking into the camp until daylight should enable me to make a general and effectual charge.' Harrison also states that his men responded quickly as veterans, though "nineteen-twentieths" had never been in an Indian battle before.

A grove of oak trees sheltered the Indians on both flanks. The left flank (the southeast angle) almost immediately caught Harrison's attention after he relieved Barton. Stationed there were the companies of Been, Snelling, and Prescott of the Fourth Regiment. There, Colonel Daviess sought permission from Harrison to charge the Indians to remove them from their sheltered position. Finally, after requesting permission three times,

Harrison allowed him to use his discretion. Daviess, dressed in a white coat, charged with only eight men and was shot down almost Instantly as the Indians fell on the flanks of his small force (he died of his wounds thirty-six hours later). Captain Josiah Snelling charged with his company and dispersed the Indians from the grove.

Next, Harrison rode over to the right flank and the right of the rear line where Captain Spier Spencer's mounted riflemen and those of Warrick's company were posted. He arrived there and asked where Spencer was. Ensign John Tipton answered him, "Dead" Harrison then asked, "Where are the lieutenants?" Again, Tipton replied, "Dead" Finally, he inquired, "Where is the ensign?" Tipton replied, "I am here." Harrison then ordered him to hold his position and promised to relieve him immediately. He immediately sent him Rob's company of regulars. Harrison commissioned Tipton, a company captain, as a reward for his excellent conduct and heroism. Harrison's men fought off at least three Indian charges, pouring a devastating fire at them with cartridges filled with twelve buckshot in each one. Concentrating at both ends of the camp, using the oak trees for cover, they rushed toward the camp in groups. The Indians fought using a rare tactic: one group would fire and retreat to load while the other group rushed forward.

As Harrison's second in command, Colonel Boyd, who began his army career as an ensign in 1786, commanded the infantry throughout the battle. He rallied the men with the words, "Hussa! My sons of gold, a few more fires, and victory will be ours." In the years after the battle, Harrison's political enemies would attribute the victory to Boyd instead of Harrison.

Harrison prepared to order charges from both sides of the perimeter at daybreak. Unaware of Harrison's plans, Major Samuel Wells led four companies in a charge on the left flank. The companies of Cook and Larabee afterward charged the Indians on the right flank. While both forces were uncoordinated in their efforts and limited in the number of cavalry, they nevertheless returned to their lines after the charge forced the Indians to flee for the safety of swamps. The now demoralized Indians realized the Prophet's promises had not protected them and, running low on ammunition, abandoned the field. Thus ended the bloody battle that had lasted for about two and a quarter hours. The Indians had fought with passionate determination, suffering an estimated twenty-five to fifty killed and seventy to eighty wounded while killing sixty-eight of Harrison's men and wounding another one hundred and twenty. One newspaper account later stated that twenty-six of the sentinels had been killed with arrows. After the battle, Harrison's men scalped almost all of the Indians they could find dead on the battlefield. The next day, the army entered the now deserted town. They found new British equipment and supplies, confirming their belief that the British were instigating the Indians against them. They also burned Prophetstown along with five thousand bushels of com and beans.

Aftermath of Tippecanoe

While some Indians deserted Tecumseh's Confederacy, many more joined him after the battle. Harrison's so-called victory was short-lived, as Prophetstown was rebuilt within a few weeks after the battle. The Kickapoos, who suffered the loss of eleven warriors in the fight, were especially hardened in their hatred of the Americans and were determined to seek revenge. That following winter and spring, Kickapoos went on a rampage in Illinois, and many settlers suffered. In the worst attack near Peoria, Kickapoos massacred ten members of the O'Neal family. Consequently, many Illinois families began to flee the territory. At the time, Ninian Edwards, governor of the Illinois Territory since 1809, estimated there were 1500 Indian warriors in Illinois and about 2000 white male citizens above the age of twenty-one.

As early as 1810, Illinois Territory residents sought assistance from the Federal government to contribute to their defenses because of the increase in Indian depredations. At a mass meeting in St. Clair County, Colonel William Whiteside, and Samuel Davidson asked Governor Edwards to forward their request to the Federal government, stating, "From different circumstances, the inhabitants of this country are not in possession of a sufficiency of arms to repel any attack that may be offered; owing to the present alarm, it is not in our power to buy any, and a considerable portion of the militia are not circumstanced to buy. If your Excellency will be pleased to make use of your good offices to obtain from the general government the use of what rifles and muskets may be thought in your wisdom needful, it certainly would be of great service to this frontier country." Congress responded by authorizing ten companies of mounted Rangers, four of which were for Illinois: Captain William Whiteside, Captain Samuel Whiteside, Captain James Moore, and Captain Jacob Short.

Indian hostility increased in early 1812, provoking three hundred settlers to leave Illinois territory in the early months of the year. The first six months of the year proved more hazardous to area settlers as more than five times the number of Americans (fifty) were killed in Illinois, Indiana, Ohio, and Louisiana than had died in 1810 and 1811. Attributable to the increases in small, sporadic, but deadly raids and attacks, Illinois residents began to "fort up in Illinois Territory before the declaration of war in 1812.

In general, those forts were block houses, built of logs, a story and a half or two stories in height, with comers closely trimmed; the walls of the first being provided with port holes and doors, the last named being made of thick puncheons, firmly fastened together and as strongly barred on the inside. The upper story projected over the lower some three feet. They were generally built into diagonally opposite comers of the stockade; sometimes, one was built in each of the four comers, and yet again, one was built in the middle of the enclosure. These stockades were constructed by setting endwise into trenches, logs, trimmed on two sides, twelve or fifteen feet high. through which port holes were cut high enough to be above the head and under which platforms were built to bring the soldier near enough to use his gun. They were expected to enclose sufficient ground to contain a person and his property. Cabins to contain all were generally erected. Wells were typically dug to provide water. Nothing needed to resist a long siege was omitted. Those posts usually afforded ample protection, and few accidents were reported by those who "forted" themselves.

Governor Edwards had already, in June of 1811, ordered the construction of blockhouses. By March of 1813, there was a chain of twenty-two blockhouses between the Mississippi and Kaskaskia Rivers. Also, in March of 1812, Congress authorized raising six U.S. ranger companies, one of which was used to guard the Illinois Territory. Edwards would also rely on the militia drawn from the roughly 12,000 inhabitants to defend Illinois Territory. The militia consisted of every white male between eighteen and forty-five. Each man had to supply his rifle or musket, bayonet, ammunition, and a knapsack.

In August 1811, Governor Edwards said at a conference with Indians in Peoria, to keep them peaceful, "My children, now open your ears to hear my words, and let them sink deep into your hearts. If you wish for peace with us, you must do us justice. If you disapprove those murders and other outrages that have been committed, you must deliver up the offenders; for if your harbor among you such deadly enemies to us, you cannot be our friends, and you ought not to expect our friendship." In another later conference in July, the Potawatomi chief: Gomo said, "Formerly, when the French were here, they made us large presents; so have the English; but the Americans, in giving their presents, have always asked a piece of land in return. Such has been the treatment of the Americans."

Expecting war to break out soon, in April 1812, Governor Edwards and Governor William Clark of Missouri Territory met again in council with the various tribes of Illinois in Cahokia. Edwards tried to discourage them from joining the British side, saying, "My children, the British pretend to be your friends, but their object is to get you to fight their battle, and they care not what becomes of you afterward." Edwards tried to reassure them about American intentions, saying, "My children, we never want to buy your land, or take it from you, unless you wish to sell it, and then we will give you the price that you ask for it" In July, Gomo spoke for the Indians, stating they desired peace, but made no specific promises.

In August 1812, Edwards told the Indians, "My children your Great Father has nothing to fear from war with you, for if it were possible for the red skins to conquer one army, he could soon have another, ten times as strong to oppose you. But he does not wish for war. You have nothing to hope from it, and you will do justice and comply with your treaty. My children, we are about to engage in a war with the British. I wish you to see how different our condition is from theirs. We do not wish you to take any part with us in the war; we do not wish you to fight for us, because we know we are able to whip them without your help; we were as children we fought, conquered them, and shook the whole United States away from them; and if we fight them again, we shall whip them and take the Canadas away from them. For this purpose our Great Father now has an army of 185,000 men. My children, the British pretend to be your friends, but their object is to get you to fight their battles; and they care not what becomes of you afterwards. They tell you of the power of their king over the great lake. They say to you, that he can conquer us, but they know this is not true. If they thought they were able to fight us, why are they so anxious to get you to assist them?"

In actuality, the Indians did not believe the Americans; they had already taken too much Indian land. Both sides had irreconcilable differences, and hostilities continued. Most of the Indians, knowing of American land hunger and swayed by British supplies and propaganda, sided with the British and waited for the announcement of war to join in the fight.

Summary Part II Revolutionary War Period

The American colonies fought the Revolutionary War to win their independence from Britain. Primarily through the conquests of George Rogers Clark, the Treaty of Paris terms awarded the United States the Northwest Territory; the young nation had to fight and negotiate with the various Indian tribes to take actual possession of the land. The Indians fought hard, winning several victories over the United States army. After Anthony Wayne defeated the Miami Confederation of Indian tribes at the Battle of Fallen Timbers in 1794, the tribes submitted to the power of the United States at the Treaty of Greenville. They would yield up their land treaty by treaty in the following years. In both the treaties of 1804 and 1809, land in Illinois was ceded to the Americans.

Though the British had finally given up the forts at Mackinac and Detroit as a condition of Jay's Treaty in 1795, they continued to supply the Indians with arms, ammunition, and other provisions. They still primarily controlled the fur trade in the Northwest Territory and promised support to the Indians when the war was renewed. The Shawnee leader Tecumseh, brother of Tenskatawawa, had begun in earnest to prepare for war after Harrison had persuaded various Indian tribes to cede three million acres of land in the 1809 treaty and especially after the Battle of Tippecanoe in November of 1811, Indian murders and harassment of settlers sharply increased. The Indian danger caused some settlers to flee Illinois Territory. By June 1812, Governor Edwards estimated that 1700 men were available for militia service, a decrease of three hundred men in just the past few months.

Tecumseh's recruiting drive in the South before the Battle of Tippecanoe was largely unsuccessful. His anger against the Americans was now at a fever pitch, yet he knew the Indians alone could not win a war against the Americans; he needed the British as active allies. The white population of the Northwest Territory in 1810 was about 270,000 compared to about 70,000 Indians. Of these Indians, trader Thomas Forsyth estimated about 5000 warriors were available, while Henry Rowe Schoolcraft thought Indian forces could be as high as 8000.

In Illinois, except Fort Dearborn, the Indians, mainly Sauk, Potawatomi, and Kickapoo, still controlled all but the southern portion of the state. However, before plunging into full-scale war with the Americans, they, Tecumseh, and his other Indian partners needed to first wait for British support. The Indians required actual British manpower and material resources to wage war. They would not have to wait much longer as events outside Illinois would bring war to its territory.

Part III
The War of 1812

Chapter Eight

Fort Dearborn

For years before 1812, the United States had suffered abuses from Great Britain, including interference with trade and impressment of American citizens into the British Navy. From 1789 to the beginning of the War of 1812, the British impressed as many as 10,000 Americans into their navy. Westerners complained loudly of the British arming and supporting the Indians and inciting them to commit hostilities. They also believed that removing the British from Canada would solve the problem and that the conquest of Canada, as former president Thomas Jefferson stated, would be a simple "matter of marching." Consequently, under President James Madison, the United States declared war on Great Britain on June 18, 1812. In August, the garrison of Fort Dearborn, located on the future site of the city of Chicago, would suffer severe and fatal consequences from that declaration.

Fort Dearborn's origin resulted from the government's need for firmer American control of the Northwest Territory, including Illinois. The Potawatomi Indians were stirring up trouble by raiding Osages and killing Americans who happened to be in the wrong place. Also, in the years following the Revolutionary War, the Americans especially desired to reduce the influence of the British, who continued to dominate the lucrative fur trade between the Great Lakes and the Mississippi. However, the

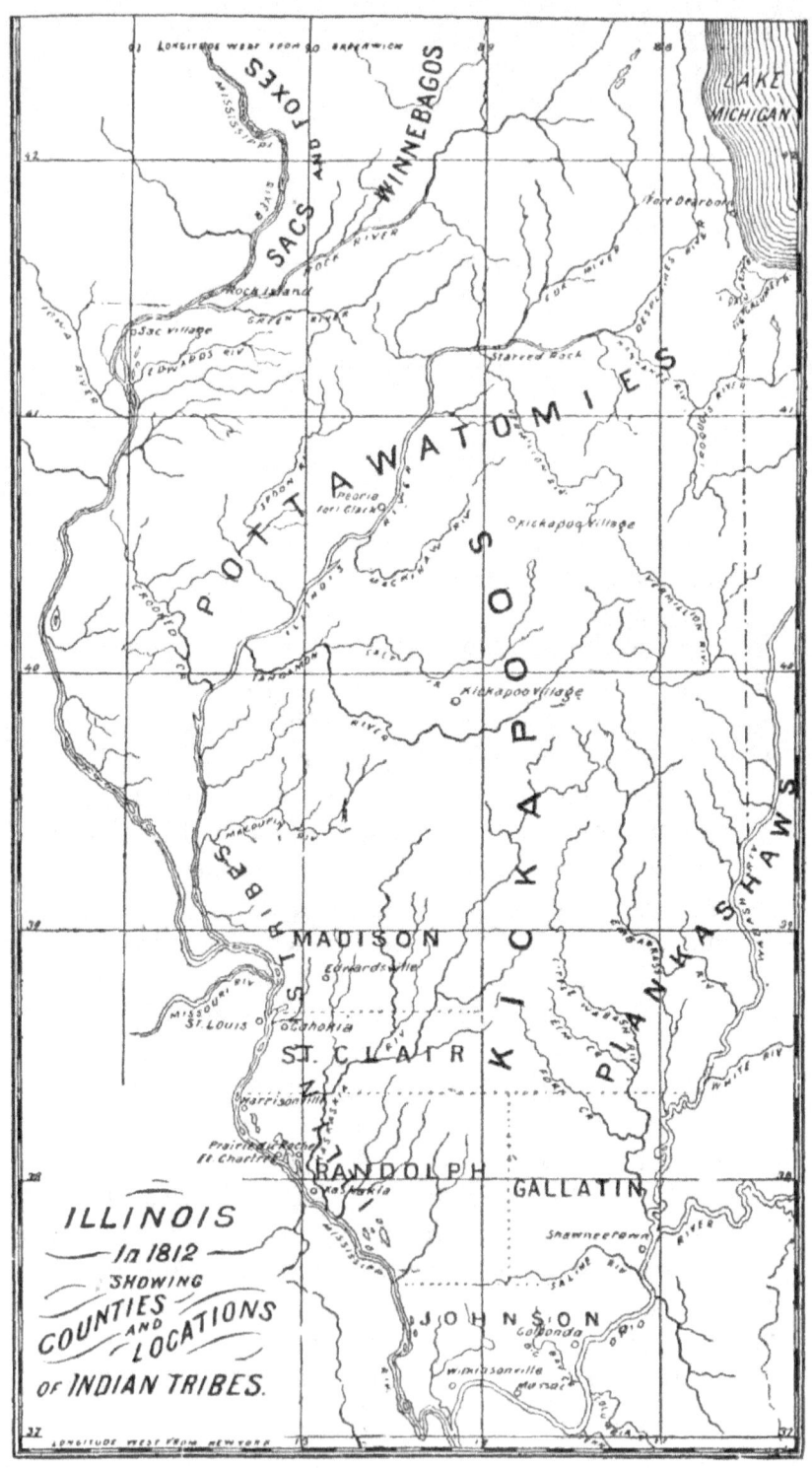

MAP OF ILLINOIS IN 1812

Showing counties and location of Indian tribes.

territory belonged to the United States.

Fort Dearborn was built near a few French-Canadian cabins, including one previously owned by the Haitian-American trader Baptiste Point Du Sable. Du Sable was the first recognized permanent American to settle in Chicago sometime in the 1780s. Notably, the French-Canadian trader John Kinzie moved into Du Sable's old cabin in 1804. Kinzie, formerly a British subject born in Quebec, operated a trading house and was well-liked and respected by the Indians.

Captain John Whistler constructed Fort Dearborn in 1803-1804 on a parcel of land given up to the United States by the Indians after their defeat at the Battle of Fallen Timbers in 1794. The fort was surrounded on three sides by a bend in the Chicago River. It had buildings enclosed by two blockhouses and a double row of high pickets. Captain Whistler commanded the fort in its first seven years until relieved by Captain Nathan Heald. Heald, who had served as Captain at Fort Wayne, arrived in mid-1810 to command the fifty-four soldiers' garrison.

After the war was declared, the Americans moved first in the Northwest Territory. Brigadier General William Hull, governor of Michigan Territory and commander of the army of the Northwest crossed the Detroit River into Canada on July 12, 1812. The British and Indians, now finally combined in their shared interest in fighting the Americans, captured Fort Mackinac on July 17. Hull had learned in late July that the British and Indians had captured Fort Mackinac. Knowing that the supply line to Fort Dearborn was now cut and fearing for the safety of the isolated fort surrounded by hostile Indians, Hull immediately sent orders to Heald to evacuate the fort and to distribute the goods stored in the government factory. Hull also sent orders to the garrison at Fort Wayne to assist Fort Dearborn in any way they could.

Heald knew the Indians in the area were hostile. Back in 1809, over one hundred Winnebago had descended on the fort in the hope of attacking it but were stymied when the Indian agent at the fort warned the troops, and the gates to the fort were shut Reports also surfaced in 1810 that Tecumseh had made plans to attack Fort Dearborn when war came. The Potawatomi were to lead the attack. More recently, on April 15, Heald reported, "The Indians have commenced hostilities in this quarter, on the 6th inst. A little before the sunset, a party of eleven Indians, supposed to be Winnebago, came to Messrs. Russell and Leigh's cabin in a field on the portage branch of the Chicago River about three miles from the garrison, where they murdered two men, one by the name of Liberty White, an American, and the other a Canadian Frenchman, whose name I do not know. White received two balls through the body, nine stabs with a knife in his breast and one in his hip; his throat was cut from ear to ear, his nose and lips were taken off in one piece, and he was skinned almost as far round as they could find any hair. The Frenchman was only shot through the neck and scalped. Since the murder of these two men, one or two other parties of Indians have been lurking about us, but we have been so much on our guard that they have not been able to get any scalps."

    Heald received the orders to evacuate the fort on August 8 from an Indian runner, the friendly Potawatomi Chief Winnemac. Winnemac advised Heald to evacuate the fort immediately before the hostile Potawatomi could gather their warriors. Heald also had orders to distribute the goods and destroy surplus arms and ammunition. In the morning following the arrival of his orders, Heald read them on the parade grounds, giving the Indians an incentive to get together immediately in anticipation of receiving booty. Heald delayed his departure for almost a week to provide time to prepare for an organized withdrawal and to distribute the goods. Unfortunately, the word of Heald's offer to distribute goods spread quickly, and great numbers of Indians eagerly gathered near the fort from villages around Lake Michigan.

The next day, a Potawatomi chief, Black Partridge (also called Black Bird), warned Heald to be careful on his march. Previously, Black Partridge had been the Americans' friend and ally. Still, on this day, he gave a medal he had received from President Madison for conspicuous services back to Heald, stating, "Rather, I come to deliver to you the medal I wear. It was given me by the Americans, and I have long worn it in token of our mutual friendship. But our young men are resolved to imbrue their hands in the blood of the whites. I cannot restrain them and I will not wear a token of peace when I am compelled to act as an enemy." Though the fort was strongly positioned and manned to withstand any Indian assault and endure a short siege, Heald believed he was obligated to obey the evacuation orders.

On August 13, Captain William Wells, Indian agent to the Miami whose sister Rebecca was married to Heald, arrived from Fort Wayne at the head of thirty to forty friendly Miami Indian warriors to accompany the garrison and civilian residents on their journey. The Potawatomi disliked Wells and viewed him as a traitor. Raised by the Miami since he was fourteen and married to a daughter of Little Turtle, Wells returned to the Americans and aided Anthony Wayne at Fallen Timbers. He also favored Little Turtle's Miami in winning concessions from the U.S. government.

Heald must have felt some sense of security as he held a council with the Indians to arrange for the distribution of goods. He also arranged for an escort to help protect his little force when he marched out (an escort of three hundred Potawatomi marched out with him). On the 14th, except for liquor, guns, and ammunition, which had all been dumped down a well and the river, Heald distributed the fort's goods. As both Wells and Kinzie advised, Heald destroyed eight hundred and fifty pounds of gunpowder and 1200 gallons of Whiskey belonging to trader John Kinzie. Unfortunately, the Indians must have believed they would receive all the goods. On the night that Heald dumped the goods, the Indians observed the destruction of the guns and liquor and brought it up at another council the next afternoon. The Indians were angered by the dumping and charged the whites with deceit.

Undoubtedly, the fact that they did not receive any liquor, guns, or ammunition served to increase the hostility of the Indians. In his autobiography, the Sauk chief Black Hawk stated that Heald had promised the local Indians that he would give them a considerable quantity of powder and that, in his opinion, the garrison would have had a safe passage if the promise had been kept.

The next day, August 15, Heald marched out with fifty-four soldiers, twelve militia, nine women, and eighteen children. After a march of about one and a half miles, the Potawatomi escort disappeared behind some ridges, rapidly five hundred Potawatomi, Ottawa, Kickapoo, and Winnebago Indians under Potawatomi Chiefs Black Partridge and Mad Sturgeon ambushed Heald's woefully outnumbered column of soldiers and civilians.

The following account of the ensuing battle is told by Milo Quaife in *Chicago and the Old Northwest 1673-1835*.

All preparations being complete, about nine o'clock the stockade gate was thrown open and there issued forth the saddest procession Michigan Avenue has ever known. In the lead were a part of the Miamis, and Wells, their leader, alert and watching keenly for the first signs of a hostile demonstration. In due array followed the garrison, the women and children who were able to walk, and the Chicago militia, the rear being brought up by the remainder of the Miamis. Most of the children, being too young to walk, rode in one of the wagons, accompanied, probably by one or more of the women. Mrs. Heald and Mrs. Helm were mounted and near or with their husbands, though each couple became separated early in the combat. The other women and children were on foot around the baggage wagons, which were guarded by Ensign Ronan, Surgeon Van Voorhis, the soldiers who had families, and the twelve Chicago militia.

The route taken was due south, parallel with the river until its mouth was reached and then along the beach, not far, probably from the present Michigan Avenue, for most of the land to the east has been filled in since the beginning of modern Chicago. On the right of the column moved an escort of Potawatomies. Below the mouth of the river began a row of sand hills, or ridges, which ran between the prairie and the beach, parallel to the latter and distant from it about one hundred yards. When these were reached the soldiers continued along the beach, while the Potawatomies disappeared behind the ridges to the right. The reason for this soon became apparent. When a distance of about a mile and a half had been traversed by the soldiers Captain Wells, who with his militia was some distance in advance, discovered that the Indians had prepared an ambush for the whites and were about to attack them from their vantage point behind the bank. Aware of a favorable position for defense a short distance ahead, he rode rapidly back toward the main body to urge Heald to press forward and occupy it, swinging his hat in a circle around his head as he went, as a signal that the party was surrounded. The heads of the warriors now became visible all along the line, popping up "like turtles out of the water." The troops immediately charged up the bank, and with a single volley followed home with a bayonet charge scattered the Indians before them. But this move proved as futile as it was brave. The Indians gave way in front only to join their fellows in another place, on the flank or in the rear, and the fight went on.

Meanwhile a deadlier combat, which we may perhaps think of as a separate battle, was raging around the wagons in the rear. Here it was that the real massacre occurred. Apparently in the charge up the sand hills and in the ensuing movements the main division of the regulars under Heald became separated from the rear division, and yet it was precisely here, where the provisions and the helpless women and children were placed, that protection was most urgently needed. The Indians, outnumbering the whites almost ten to one, swarmed around, some apparently, even coming from the front to share in the easier contest at this point. Here were the junior officers, Ronan and Van Voorhis, and here, apparently, Kinzie had elected to stay. Around the wagons too were the militia, twelve in number, compromising the male inhabitants of the settlement capable of bearing arms, who had been organized and armed by Heald at the time of the April murders. The combat here was furious, being waged hand to hand in an indiscriminate melee. Fighting desperately with bayonet and musket-butt the militia were cut down to a man. But one, Sergeant Burns, escaped instant death, and he, grievously wounded, was slaughtered an hour after the surrender by an infuriated squaw. Ronan and Van Voorhis shared their fate as did the regular soldiers, Kinzie being the only white man at the wagons who survived. Even the soldiers' wives, armed with swords, hacked bravely away as long as they were able. In the course of the melee two of the women and most of the children were slain.

The butchery of these unfortunate innocents constitutes the saddest feature of that gory day. The measure which had been taken to insure their welfare was responsible for their destruction; for while the conflict raged hotly, a young fiend broke through the defenders of the wagons and climbing into the one containing the children quickly tomahawked all but one of them. Of the women slain one was Mrs. Corbin, the wife of a private soldier, who is said to have resolved never to be taken prisoner, dreading more than death the indignities she believed would be in store for her. Accordingly she fought until she was cut to pieces. The other was Cicely, Mrs. Heald's negro serving woman. She and her infant son, who all perished afford two of the few instances of which we have authentic record of negroes being held in slavery at Chicago.

While this slaughter was going on at the wagons Captain Wells, who had been fighting in front with the main body of troops, seems to have started back to the scene to engage in a last effort to save the women and children. His horse was wounded and he himself was shot through the breast. He bade his niece farewell, when his horse fell, throwing him prostrate on the ground with one leg caught under its side. Some Indians approaching, he continued to fire at them, killing one or more from his prostrate position. An Indian now took aim at him, seeing which Wells signed to him to shoot, and his stormy career was ended. The foe paid their sincerest tribute of respect to his bravery by cutting out his heart and eating it, thinking thus to imbibe the qualities of its owner in life. Wells was the real hero of the Chicago massacre, giving his life voluntarily to save his friends. The debt which Chicago owes to his memory an earlier generation sought to discharge by giving his name to one of the city's principal streets. But to its shame a later one robbed him in large part of this honor, by giving to that portion of the street which runs south of the river the inappropriate and meaningless designation of Fifth Avenue.

    The close of another brave career was dramatic enough to deserve separate mention. During the battle Sergeant Hayes, who had already manifested the greatest bravery, engaged in individual combat with an Indian. The guns of both had been discharged, when the Indian ran up to him with uplifted tomahawk. Before the warrior could strike Hayes ran his bayonet into his breast up to the socket, so that he could not pull it out. In this situation, supported by the bayonet, the Indian tomahawked him, and the foemen fell dead together, the bayonet still in the red man's breast.

    Meanwhile what of Captain Heald and the troops under his immediate direction? The Miamis had abandoned the Americans at the first sign of hostilities. After a few minutes of sharp fighting Heald drew off with such of his men as still survived to a slight elevation on the open prairie, out of shot of the bank or any other cover. Here he enjoyed a temporary respite, for the Indians refrained from following him, having no desire, apparently, to grapple with the regulars at close range in the open. The fight thus far had lasted only about fifteen minutes, yet half of the regulars had fallen, Wells and two of the officers were dead and the other two wounded, and the Americans were hopelessly beaten. The alternatives before them were to die fighting to the last, or to surrender and trust to the savages for mercy. After some delay the Indians sent a half-breed interpreter, who lived near the fort and was friendly with the garrison, and who in the commencement of the action had gone over to the Indians in the hope of saving his life, to make overtures for a surrender. Heald advanced alone toward the Indians and was met by the interpreter and the chief, Black Bird, who requested him to surrender, promising to spare the lives of the prisoners. The soldiers at first opposed the proposition, but after some parleying the surrender was made, Captain Heald promising, as a further inducement to the Indians to spare the prisoners, a ransom of one hundred dollars for every one still living. The captives were now led back to the beach and thence along the route toward the fort over which they had passed but an hour or so before. On the way they passed the scene of the massacre around the wagons. Helm records his horror at the sight of the men, women, and children "lying naked with principally all their heads off." In passing the bodies he thought he perceived that of his wife, with her head severed from her shoulders. The sight almost overcame him, and we may readily believe that "now began to repent" that he had ever surrendered. He was happily surprised, however, on approaching the fort to find her alive and well, sitting crying among some squaws. She owed her preservation to the friendly Black Partridge, who had claimed her as his prisoner.

In the action the white force numbered fifty-five regulars and twelve militia in addition to Wells and Kinzie, the latter of whom did not participate in the fighting. Against these were pitted about five hundred Indians. The white men were better armed, but the Indians had the advantage of position and of freedom from the incumbrance of baggage and women and children to protect. Under the circumstances the odds were overwhelmingly in their favor, and their comparatively easy victory was but matter of course. Their loss was estimated by Heald at about fifteen. The Americans killed in the action comprised twenty-six regular soldiers, the twelve militia and Captain Wells, with two of the women and twelve children. A number of the survivors, too, were wounded.

Following the surrender came the customary scenes of savage cruelty. The friendly Indians could answer only for the prisoners in their possession. Some of the wounded were tortured to death, and it is not improbable that some of the prisoners were burned at the stake. For the remainder of the day and the ensuing night the victors surfeited themselves with the plunder and the torture. The following day the plundering of the fort and the distribution of the prisoners were completed, the buildings were fired, and the bands set out for their several villages.

Through the efforts of the British enemy, mainly the influential fur trader Robert Dickson, General Henry Proctor, and Captain Roberts at Mackinac, eventually, about half of the captives were freed from captivity, including Captain Heald and his wife, Lieutenant Helm and his wife, and the Kinzie family. Approximately twenty-nine soldiers, seven women, and six children survived the massacre. Nine men who survived were finally released almost two years later. They were James Van Horn, Dyson Dyer, Joseph Noles, Joseph Bowen, Paul Grumm, Nathan Edson, Elias Mills, Janes Corbin, and Fielding Corbin.

Under the overall instruction of Tecumseh, the Indians soon turned their attention to other forts in the region. Soon after the Fort Dearborn massacre, attacks were made on Forts Wayne and Harrison in the Indiana Territory and Fort Madison in the Missouri Territory.

Indians attacked Fort Wayne twice unsuccessfully in early September. During the brief siege, they fashioned two logs in the shape of a cannon. They then informed Captain James Rhea that the British had supplied them with the cannon and that they would massacre the entire garrison when additional Indians arrived the next day if the fort was not immediately surrendered. Having been informed by a messenger who had been able to elude the Indians and enter the fort that General William Henry Harrison was on his way with a 2000-man army to relieve the fort, Rhea ignored the Indian demand. The Indians then withdrew after one week.

Also, in the early days of September, several hundred Indians assaulted Fort Harrison. They burned a blockhouse down, exposing a twenty-foot gap in the fort's wall. Captain Zachary Taylor's men managed to contain the fire, erected temporary breastworks, and repelled the attack. Two messengers evaded the surrounding and besieging Indians and reached Vincennes, where they delivered a message requesting help. When a force of 1000 assorted volunteers, rangers, and militia descended on the fort after it had suffered through a thirteen-day siege, the Indians were gone. The offensive action was not entirely one-sided. That fall, Harrison's forces burned over twenty Indian villages in Northern Indiana and Southern Michigan.

Chapter Nine

Fort Madison

Before the War of 1812, the combined Sauk and Fox tribes occupied land in Western Illinois, Western Iowa, and Southern Wisconsin. They ruled the territory bounded roughly by the Wisconsin River on the north, about the middle of present-day Illinois on the east, the Missouri River on the south, and the watershed between the De Moines and Missouri River on the west. Their principal village of Saukenuk near present-day Rock Island, Illinois, may have been the largest town in Illinois Territory then. They were hostile to the Americans. This was mainly due to a treaty signed with William Henry Harrison in November 1804 by five Sauk and Fox chiefs, who did not have the authority to do so.

The chiefs had come to St. Louis to rectify a potential crisis created by a few Sauk braves who had murdered two Americans during the summer. President Thomas Jefferson seized the opportunity to gain control over land that the tribes occupied in Northern Illinois and Southern Wisconsin and to reduce the activities of British agents and traders. Secretary of War Henry Dearborn instructed Harrison to seek land cessions from the tribes. A message written by the United States Indian agent at St. Louis did not indicate to the chiefs that they would negotiate a treaty. He wrote them as follows:

> My brothers. The great chief of the seventeen great cities of America, having chosen me to maintain peace and union between all the

Redskins and the government of the United States, I have, in consequence just received the order for the great Chief of our country, who has just arrived from the post of Vincennes, to send for the chiefs of your villages with some important men, and to bring with them those of you who recently killed his children; I urge you to come at once, and if some great reasons prevent you from bringing the murderers with you, this is not to prevent you from obeying the orders which I transmit to you. When you carry them out, you will be treated as chiefs, and you will go home after having listened to the word of your Father, and then you can make it understood by your elders and your young people, so open your ears and come at once. You will be treated as friends and allies of the United States.

Upon their arrival, the delegation of Quashquame, Pashipaho, and three others turned over one of the murderers and then tried to pay Harrison for his release. However, Harrison only agreed to meet their demand after a land cession. Having liberally supplied the chiefs with whiskey, Harrison persuaded them to sign away over fifteen million acres of land in a portion of Missouri, Illinois, and Wisconsin. It has been called one of the cheapest land acquisitions by the United States in the Old Northwest Territory. The treaty's terms allowed the tribes to remain on the land until the government sold it, yet the Indians would eventually have to move across the west side of the Mississippi River. In addition to the more than $2,000 spent on the tribal delegation in St. Louis, the government would pay annuities of $1,000 a year, supply the services of a trader and a blacksmith, and send someone to teach them how to farm, all in all, a terrific bargain for the United States.

In reality, no one truly knows what happened during the negotiation of the 1804 treaty. After the Sauk and Fox learned they would lose their land, about one hundred fifty of them traveled to St. Louis in 1805 to complain. The new governor, General James Wilkinson, distributed more gifts and tried to assure them that the United States would not intrude onto their territory. However, they left very embittered and distrustful of the Americans.

By the beginning of the War of 1812, the Sauk already had a tumultuous relationship with the Americans at Fort Madison. The Sauk had learned In the Spring of 1808 that the Americans were building a fort at the rapids of the Des Moines River. Sauk visited the fort to see if its location violated the 1804 treaty. When they held a council, it was agreed that there was no violation (Black Hawk excepted). Later in the year, a potentially violent incident was narrowly avoided when Black Hawk and some warriors visited. By one account, in April, the Indians appeared on the bank across the river from the fort. Several men warned the commander, First Lieutenant Alpha Kingsley, that the Indians planned mischief, and young Ioway brave, whom the fort sutler had befriended at Detroit, warned that an attack would soon be made. Forewarned, Kingsley avoided a treacherous attack when he refused Black Hawk and Chief Pashepaho's request to enter the fort and do a dance for the soldiers. The chiefs had complained that the ground outside the fort was too rough and bumpy for such a dance.

According to Black Hawk's autobiography, no premeditated attack had been planned on the fort. Instead, he claimed that a group of men (including himself) went to the fort to see what the soldiers were doing. After a while, some of the young braves followed an armed work party from the fort. Once they set down their guns and went to work with axes, some of the Indians sneaked up and stole the guns, and then they gave a yell. The soldiers threw down their axes and ran for their weapons. At this point, the young braves surrounded them, laughed at the soldiers, and returned the guns. Because of this incident, the fort commander called for a council with the Indians. All the Indians gathered around the fort, which had low walls at the time. At the head of the dancing braves, Black Hawk approached the fort and requested entrance to perform a dance for the soldiers. Kingsley, already on the alert for trouble, had his soldiers ready with arms, one standing by the previously loaded cannon with a match ready to fire. Speaking through an interpreter, Kingsley said, "Tell Chief Pashepaho that the first man who steps over the gate will be fired upon. That is my answer to his request." Subsequently, the Braves turned away, raised the war clubs concealed under blankets, yelled out war cries in frustration, and quickly left. One witness noted that "in twenty minutes, not an Indian was to be seen on the north side of the river." Black Hawk later admitted that if they had entered the fort, they probably would have killed the entire garrison, as had once been done at Fort Michilimackinac during Pontiac's Conspiracy.

  Kingsley then completed the fort, which consisted of a one hundred and twenty square foot palisade and contained two-story blockhouses on each corner. The fort was located on a safe elevation about twenty-five feet from the Mississippi River. A ridge behind the fort dominated its position; this would prove fatal to its future occupancy. A government "factory" building (trading post) was built outside the fort. The Indians brought furs, skins, and bars of lead from the lead mines (where Dubuque, Iowa, is now located) to the factory in exchange for blankets, needles, muskets, tomahawks, knives, fish hooks, cooking pots, and many other items desired by the Indians. The fort trading "factor" John Johnson recorded that in 1809, he received from the Indians in trade two hundred and seventy-four deerskin packs, seven packs of beaver furs, and seventeen packs of bearskins, among other items. In 1810, Johnson acquired 80,000 pounds of lead from the Indians.

In late June 1812, a Kickapoo chief representing the Shawnee Prophet brought a red wampum belt inviting the Indians of nine nations to gather for council at Saukenuk to go to war against the Americans. One faction of the Sauk joined the Winnebago in attacking Fort Madison. Lieutenant Thomas Hamilton, now in command, had received prior notice of an impending attack when a party of thirty Sauk warned him. Hamilton had also learned on August 24 of the fall of Fort Dearborn. Hamilton then requested reinforcements from Colonel Daniel Bissell. Captain Horatio Stark arrived with nineteen men and assumed command of the fort three days before the Indians attacked on September 5.

As Black Hawk related, he joined a Winnebago war party that had decided to attack the fort. The Indians sent spies out and observed that only fifty men occupied the fort. They concealed themselves near the fort at night and planned to rush in when the gate was opened, and a signal was given. They had previously observed the entire garrison frequently drilling outside, which would surprise them then. After daybreak, one young man walked out of the fort to the river and returned, but Black Hawk did not rush the gate because he feared his party was not ready. A short time later, four men left the fort and walked down to the river to gather wood. While they were gone, Private John Cox then came out, and when he was only twenty-five feet outside the fort walls, a Winnebago fired on him, killed him, and scalped him. The other men heard the firing and ran toward the fort; two of them did not make it back. Black Hawk and the other warriors shot at the fort all day. Later, Black Hawk recounted an event on the second day when he shot the flag post in two, thus preventing the soldiers from raising it. He omitted the fact that it took a reported four hundred shots to bring the flag down finally. On the same day, the Indians also killed all of the cattle, hogs, and chickens that the garrison kept outside the stockade. The next day, they impaled Private Cox's head and heart on stakes buried in the mud near the river.

During the siege, the Indians tried unsuccessfully to set the fort on fire but were thwarted by the soldiers who kept the shingles too wet to ignite and kept putting out other fires by utilizing old muskets as "squirts." Fearful that the Indians may be able to burn the fort down by starting the trading house on fire when the wind was blowing toward the fort, Lieutenant Hamilton sent a soldier to start it on fire during a lull in the fighting. Slipping through the garden when the wind was calm, the soldier succeeded in his mission, and the house burned down without harming the fort. The loss in trade goods in the fire amounted to $5,500, including one hundred and twenty bear skins worth $10 each.

The Indians controlled a ridge that overlooked Fort Madison, from which they could rain down musket balls or arrows at anyone who moved from blockhouse to blockhouse. Despite this advantage, they succeeded in only wounding one of the garrison in their shooting. They broke the siege on September 9 when they ran out of ammunition.

Sometime after the Indian attack, Stark sought permission to abandon the fort. However, Governor Howard wanted it to remain. In May, Stark again left command of the fort to Hamilton. During the summer of 1813, Hamilton started construction of a blockhouse by a ravine that the Indians had used for shelter during the attack the previous year to improve the fort's defenses further. On July 8, Sauk and Winnebago warriors killed two men and wounded one of a fatigue party cutting logs for the new blockhouse.

In another attack on the morning of July 15, Indians killed four more men who were guarding the still uncompleted blockhouse. In response, soldiers fired a cannon from one of the fort's blockhouses, injuring and driving the attackers away. The Indians continued their assault until dusk by firing down on the stockade from a ridge behind the fort.

Two days after the fight, Hamilton sent a letter to Colonel Bissell at Fort Belle Fontaine stating, "A man is positively in danger of losing his life to be seen outside the garrison." Hamilton wrote that he would take responsibility for abandoning the fort if he did not hear from Bissell in a month. On the night of September 3, Hamilton burned and abandoned the fort. His men crawled down an escape trench to the Mississippi River and pulled away in two keelboats. At the time of departure, about one hundred men had garrisoned the fort.

Chapter Ten

Peoria

Peoria: Edwards Expedition

In September 1812, the Potawatomi chief, Main Poc, sent messages to the Illinois River Indians requesting them to join the war. The British had achieved a great victory at Detroit by forcing William Hull to surrender an army of 2500 men. Now was the time to act to push the Americans off of Indian land. In response, about four hundred Potawatomi, Kickapoo, and Piankashaw warriors from the Peoria area moved down the Illinois River to attack southern Illinois settlements. However, after encountering and skirmishing with some Missouri Rangers, they fled to their villages.

Desiring to forestall future attacks, Governor Edwards gathered three hundred men for an expedition against the Peoria Lake villages. Edwards's appointment as governor ended on June 21; however, he had not received any notice of a replacement. He funded the expedition from his resources, as the militiamen who had already served had not been paid. Before the expedition left, Captain William Russell arrived from Vincennes with about fifty regulars. Russel informed Edwards that Major General Samuel Hopkins, head of 2000 Kentucky volunteers, planned to lead his men against the Indian villages around Peoria and would arrive about the same time as Edwards. Edwards then sent Captain Craig, with one company of volunteers and two boats, to Peoria with tools to construct a fort when Hopkins arrived. Edward's then proceeded to attack the Indian villages around Peoria. On this expedition, Edwards would destroy five Potawatomi, Kickapoo, and Miami villages.

His account of the attack on the Indian Villages written on Nov. 18, 1812, "To the Hon. Wm. Eustis, Secretary of War, Washington City, is as follows:

>On the 18th of October, having made arrangements for the defense of the frontier in my absence, and leaving a force, which under existing circumstances, I deemed adequate to that object, I commenced my march with about 400 mounted volunteers. On our way, we burnt two Kickapoo villages, on the Saline fork of Sangamon river-till which time I had permitted it to be understood that I intended to march to Peoria and cross the Illinois at that place. But as my plan was entirely a different one, I then thought it advisable to call a council of officers and unfold to them my real views and intentions, in which, they all concurring, we marched with uncommon rapidity to a large village at the head of Peoria lake, inhabited by Kickapoos and Miamis (the Miamis were actually Piankashaws). It was situated at the foot of a hill, which terminates the low grounds of the Illinois river at that place and runs many miles parallel with it. In front of this village, the bottom, which is three miles wide, is so flat, wet and marshy, as to be almost utterly impassable to man or horse. Unfortunately our guides, instead of leading us down the hill at the village, as I had expected, led us into the bottom about three quarters of a mile below it, and thereby deranged a plan of attack which I had at first contemplated As we approached the town, the Indians were seen running out of it in considerable numbers, and for some time I thought

they were forming to give us battle.

With the center of my little army I was marching in a direct course towards them, the right wing being ordered to gain their flank on the right of us, whilst the left was directed to cut off their retreat to the river. But in a short time, I discovered them, some on horseback, others on foot all running as fast as they could at right angles from that which I was pursuing, towards a point of woods in which I expected they intended to form. I immediately changed my course, ordered and led on a general charge upon them, and would have succeeded in cutting off their retreat had it not been for the unsoundness of the ground over which we had to run. We, however, rushed upon them with such impetuosity that they were forced to scatter and take refuge in the swamp, in which those who were on horseback left their horses so completely mired that they could not move. A part was pursued through the swamp to the river, where several were killed and the town of Chequeboc (a Pottawatomi chief: who headed the party that came down to attack us) together with all the provisions and other property it contained, was burnt. Another party was pursued into the swamp in a different direction; several were killed, but finally they rallied at that point in such numbers that those who pursued them were forced to retreat. I then sent in a reinforcement, which induced the Indians entirely to give ground. The pursuit and fight over, we returned to the village, which with a great quantity of provisions and other valuable Indian property, we burnt and otherwise destroyed. We brought off with us about 80 head of horses and four prisoners, having killed, according to the Indian accounts, frequently given between 24 and 30 Indians, without the loss of a single man, and having only one wounded; which in my opinion was entirely owing to the charge that was made upon the enemy, as they were run so hard that when they attempted to form, they were out of breath, and could not shoot with sufficient accuracy.

Not meeting with, nor hearing from Hopkins, and knowing that my force was too weak and our horses too much fatigued to attempt anything further, I detached a party the next day to Peoria to leave directions for the captain who commanded the boats to return as speedily as possible. This party burnt another village that had been lately built within half a mile of Peoria, by the Miamies; and we all returned to my headquarters, at Camp Russell, after a tour of thirteen days only.

After the destruction of their village, many of the Kickapoo moved to the Rock River and a site on the Iroquois River about five miles south of its mouth on the Kankakee River. The Potawatomi relocated further up the Illinois River. Both tribes had lost a significant amount of supplies to the plundering Americans, including about one thousand bushels of corn, guns, gunpowder, flints, furs, and other items.

When Craig arrived in Peoria, he saw no sign of Edwards or Hopkins and decided to wait. At Peoria, he found the village of perhaps two hundred French inhabitants largely deserted, so he allowed his men to gather and take from inhabited stores and dwellings. What happened next is related by Nehemiah Matson who years later interviewed survivors Antoine Le Clair and Hypolite Pilette. Matson's account, which is based on their statements, is as follows:

Craig's Destruction of Peoria

On Sunday morning November 5, 1812, as the people of Peoria were assembled at church, engaged in saying mass, they were startled by the report of a cannon. The congregation, partly through fright and partly curiosity, ran out of the church, where they discovered four armed boats in the lake under full sail. On coming opposite the town, the boats rounded to and landed at the wharf. Father Racine came down from the pulpit, and in his long black robe, with his bald head uncovered, started for the landing, followed by his congregation, men, women and children. Here they were met by Captain Craig and some of his men, who had landed from the boats. Thomas Forsyth, who spoke English, inquired of the commanding officer, Captain Craig, the object of his mission, but he evaded answering the question, and in return demanded of the citizens a supply of meat and vegetables for his men, which were furnished to them.

The soldiers landed from the boats and scattered through the town in search of plunder, and committed many depredations on the people. They broke open the store of Felix Fontain, in which Antoine LeClair was a clerk, and took from there two casks of wine, and drank their contents. Many of the soldiers got drunk, forced their way into dwellings, insulting women, carrying off eatables, blankets, and everything which they took a fancy to. It was long after dark before Captain Craig succeeded in getting his drunken disorderly crew on board, when the boats were pushed off from shore to prevent further depredations on the citizens. The boats lay at anchor off in the lake in order to prevent the soldiers from again visiting the town, as a precaution against an attack from the Indians.

During the night a high wind arose, and to escape the waves in the lake the boats raised their anchors and dropped down into the channel of the river, about one-half mile below the town, where they remained until morning. About daylight, eight or ten guns were fired in quick succession in the thick river timber close to the boats. Captain Craig thinking that they were attacked by Indians, ordered the boats to push out into the channel of the river, while the cannons were brought to bear and several shots fired into the timber in order to dislodge the supposed Indians.

About daybreak on the morning of the supposed attack on the boats, a party of French at the village, consisting of eight or ten in number, went out in the river timber to shoot some beeves. The cattle being mixed with buffalo would live during the winter without feeding and became partly wild, so they were frequently hunted down in the woods the same as deer. This party of hunters had attacked the herd in their lair, near where the boats of Captain Craig were at anchor, shot three beeves, and had commenced skinning them when the timber was riddled with cannon shot. The hunters became frightened, left their beeves undressed, and in great haste returned to town without having the slightest idea from what cause these hostile demonstrations were made by the troops.

A council of war was held among the officers, all of whom were in favor of burning the town, and taking the men prisoners of war, as they had without doubt pointed out the location of the boosts to the Indians, and therefore were accessory to the attack. The boats were run up to the town, when Captain Craig, with an armed force visited each house and took all the heads of families prisoners. Some of the men were still in bed, and not allowed time to dress, but hurried off to the boats with their clothing in their hands. A torch was applied to every house, and these with their contents were burned.

Women and children, with wild screams escaped from the burning buildings, and like a herd of frightened deer collected on a vacant lot back of the town The church, which contained a golden image and a crucifix, with other valuable religious emblems, a present from the Bishop of Quebec, was burned. The wind-mill, which stood on the bank of the lake and filled with grain and flour belonging to the citizens, was burned, as well as stables, stock-yards, com-cribs, Etc.

Felix Fontain, Michael LaCroix, Antoine Des Champs and Thomas Forsyth, all of whom were traders, with their stores filled with goods, which was consumed by the flames. An old man named Benit, formerly a trader, who had saved a large amount of gold by the toil of half a century, which he had laid away for old age. This gold was secreted in his dwelling, but finding it on fire he rushed in to save his treasure, and perished in the flames, and his bones were found among the ashes on the following spring by a party of hunters who visited Peoria Mrs. LaCroix, a lady of refinement and of great personal attraction, who in after years became the wife of Governor Reynolds, being alone with four small children when her house was set on fire, appealed to the soldiers to save the clothes of herself and little ones but her appeal was in vain, and with her children only she escaped from the burning building.

There is an incident connected with the burning of Peoria which to some extent explains the barbarous conduct of the soldiers, and somewhat palliates this offense against humanity. About two months before Peoria was burned, General Howard, then stationed at Portage du Sioux, sent one of his soldiers, a young half-breed named Snipkins to Peoria, in order to ascertain if the French were assisting the Indians in carrying on war against the settlements, as had been reported. This messenger, by courtesy, was called Howard's express, but in fact was a spy, learning all he could from the citizens without letting his business be known. This young scapegrace, instead of returning to the army and reporting the true state of affairs, according to orders, became enamored with a girl and prolonged his stay until the arrival Captain Craig. And to escape punishment for disobeying orders, he reported to the troops under Captain Crag that he was detained by the people of Peoria against his will, being a prisoner in their hands, which was afterwards shown to be false. If this messenger had returned to the army, and reported as he was ordered to do, Craig's expedition would have been abandoned, and the destruction of Peoria averted.

A short time before Peoria was burned, Thomas Forsyth was appointed a government agent, but this appointment was kept a secret by the department at Washington, as it was thought, if known, it would lessen his influence with the Indians, and probably prejudice his townsmen against him. When Forsyth was made a prisoner he showed his commission under the United States seal to Captain Craig, but the incredulous captain pronounced it a forgery.

When the destruction of Peoria was completed, the boats started down the river on their return homeward, carrying with them all the men as prisoners of war. Two miles below the present site of Alton, in the thick river timber, these prisoners were set at liberty, without tents, provisions, or means of returning to their families.

The women and children having been left at the burned town without food or shelter, were therefore in a suffering condition, and without assistance they could not be relieved from their helpless situation. It was now late in the fall, the sky overcast with gray clouds, and the cold November winds howled through the forest trees. While in the midst of trouble they discovered a lone Indian walking leisurely along the beach of the lake, and with a firm step approaching them.

After Captain Craig's force departed in the boats, Gomo and two warriors emerged from hiding to assist their distressed friends. Gomo and his warriors furnished the women and children with necessities and sent them downstream in canoes. After many days of exposure to cold and rain, the women and children reached Cahokia, where friends took them in. Afterward, their husbands and fathers joined them.

Hopkins Expedition

Before Edwards attacked the Peoria Lake Indians, Major General Samuel Hopkins moved across the Illinois prairie with 2000 Kentucky volunteers. Unfortunately, his army only carried provisions for ten days and lost their way. He never made it to Peoria. Under continual harassment by Kickapoo warriors, the discouraged army gave up the mission before accomplishing much of anything. What follows is Hopkins' account of the expedition:

The army having finished crossing the Wabash on the 14th inst., marched about three miles and encamped. I here requested the attendance of the general and field officers and captains, to whom I imparted the objects of the expedition and the advantages that might result from a fulfillment of them. The nearest Kickapoo villages were from eighty to one hundred miles distant, and the Peoria not more than one hundred and sixty. By breaking up these or as many as our resources would permit, we would be rendering a service to all the territories. That from their numbers, this tribe was more favorable than any near us; and from their situation and hostility, had it more in their power to do us mischief; of course to chastise and destroy these, would be rendering real benefit to our country. It was observed by some officers, that they would meet the next morning, consult together and report to me their opinions; desiring at the same time to be furnished with the person on whom I had relied for intelligence of the country.

This council was held, and all the intelligence furnished that bad been requested, and I had a report highly favorable to the enterprise. This to me was more gratifying, as early as our encampment at Vincennes, discontents and murmurings, that portended no wish to proceed further. At Busseron, I found an evident increase of discontent, although no army was ever better or more amply supplied with rations and forage than at this place. At Fort Harrison, where we encamped on the 10th, and where we were well supplied with forage, ETC., I found on the 12th and 13th many breaking off and returning without applying to me for a discharge, and as far as I know, without any notification to their officers: Indeed, I have every reason to suppose the officers of every grade, gave no countenance to such a procedure.

Thinking myself now secure in the confidence of my brother officers and the army, we proceeded on our march early on the 15th, and continued it four days, our course near north in the prairie until we came to an Indian house, where some corn, etc., had been cultivated. The last day of the march to this place, I bad been made acquainted with a return of that spirit of discontent, that had, as I had hoped subsided, and when I had ordered a halt near sun set (for the first time that day) in a fine piece of grass in the prairie, to aid our horses, I was addressed in the most rude and dictatorial manner, requiring me immediately to resume my march, or his battalion would break from the army and return! This was a Major Singleton! I mention him in justice to the other officers of that grade. But from every information, I began to fear the army waited but for a pretext to return! This was afforded next day by our guides who had thought they had discerned an Indian village on the side of a grove about ten miles from where we encamped on the fourth night of our march, and turned us about six or eight miles out of our way. An almost universal discontent seemed to prevail, and we took our course in such a direction as we hoped would best atone for the error of the morning. About or after sun set, we came to a thin grove affording water; here we took up our camp; and about this time arose one of the most violent gusts of wind, I ever remember to have seen, not proceeding from clouds. The Indians had set fire to the prairie, which drove on us so furiously, that we were compelled to fire around our camp to protect ourselves. This seems to have decided the army to return: I was informed of it so many ways, that early in the next morning (October 20th), I requested the attendance of the general and field officers, and stated to them my apprehensions, the expectations of our country, the disgrace attending the measure, and the approbation of our own consciences. Against this, I stated the weary situation of our horses and the want of provisions (which to me seemed only partial, six days having only passed since every part of the army, as was believed, was furnished with two days in bacon, beef or bread stuff) the reasons given for returning; I requested the commandants of each regiment to convene the whole of the officers belonging to it, and to take fully the sense of the army on this measure; report to commandants of brigades, who were requested to report to me in writing; adding that if 500 volunteers would turn out, I would put myself at their head and proceed in quest of the towns; and the balance of the army might retreat in safety to Fort Harrison. In less than one hour the report was made almost unanimously to return. I then requested that I might dictate the course to be pursued that day only, which I pledged myself should not put them more than six miles out of the way, my object being to cover the reconnoitering parties, I wished to send out for the discovery of the Indian towns.

About this time, the troops being paraded, I put myself in front, took my course and directed them to follow me; the columns moving off quite a contrary way. I sent Captain Taylor and Major Lee to apply to the officers leading the columns, to turn them. They were told it was not in their power. The army had taken their course and would pursue it. Discovering great confusion and disorder in the march, I threw myself in the rear, fearing an attack on those who were there from necessity, and continued in that position the whole day. The exhausted state of the horses, nor the hunger of the men retarded this day's march; so swiftly was it prosecuted that it was long before the rear arrived at the encampment.

The generals Ray, Ramsey and Allen, lent all of their aid and authority in restoring our march to order and so far succeeded, as to bring on the whole with much less loss than I had feared; indeed I have no reason think we were either followed or menaced by an enemy. I think we marched at least 80 or 90 miles in the heart of the enemy's country. Had he possessed a design to fight us, opportunities in abundance presented. So formidable was our appearance in the prairie and in the country (as I am told) never trod before by hostile feet, must impress the bordering tribes with a sense of their danger. I fit operates beneficially in this way, our labor will not be altogether vain.

As a result of both raids, the Indians had moved further away from American settlements, and for the rest of the war, only small bands with no more than thirty warriors would raid the settlers. By the end of 1812, all the tribes in Illinois Territory were at war with the Americans, except most of the Sauk and Fox and the few remaining Kaskaskia.

The war in 1813 and the Howard-Peoria Campaign

Illinois would be spared any large-scale Indian attacks in 1813 primarily due to the actions of the British agent Robert Dickson. Dickson distributed large quantities of trade goods to the Indians to win them over to the British. He also argued with them that if the British could defeat the Americans in the East, they would have to retreat behind the Greenville treaty line of 1795. At a council of tribes at the ruins of Fort Dearborn, Dickson told the gathering that 1500 Ottawa and Chippewa had already gone to Detroit to fight with the British. Persuaded by Dickson, many Potawatomi, Winnebago, Kickapoo, and some of the Sauk Indians from Illinois traveled east to join General Henry Proctor's invasion of Ohio.

Black Hawk was already a famous war chief of the Sauk. He had killed his first enemy at the age of fifteen and, by his own account, had led many war parties, killing three, seven, and as many as thirteen enemies in a single battle. After being given arms, ammunition, and other presents, he joined five hundred other Indians in going to Detroit. From Detroit, the Indians helped the British achieve victory over General James Winchester at the River Raisin in January 1813. That summer, the Indians observed the Americans defeat Proctor's attacks on Fort Meigs and Fort Stephenson. With this discouraging turn of events, many Indians deserted the British army. When General William Henry Harrison defeated General Proctor and killed Tecumseh at the Battle of the Thames in October, a portion of the Potawatomi signed an armistice with the Americans.

Meanwhile, Brigadier General Benjamin Howard, now the Illinois and Missouri Territories military commander, conducted the only campaign in Illinois in 1813. Howard planned an expedition against the Potawatomi Indians, who had started settling back at Peoria Lakes by July. Howard believed that many of the small-scale Indian attacks and raids occurring in Missouri and Southern Illinois originated in the Peoria area. Howard started his force of about 1400 men toward the villages in September.

One incident is of historical interest due to the person involved. Major Nathan Boone, Daniel Boone's youngest brother, led sixteen Rangers to scout the land route that Howard's army would take. One night, a sentinel discovered Indians stealthily surrounding their camp and withdrawing his men away from the campfires; Boone hid his men behind trees. One of Boone's men encountered an Indian during the withdrawal. They both fired at each other. At the sound of the guns, the Indians rushed the camp from one side of the woods. Most of Boone's men could not fire the wet guns. So, Boone ordered them to withdraw slowly. Boone fell into a sinkhole as he moved backward, just before the Indians fired a volley that probably would have killed him. The Indians then broke off the attack to steal the Ranger's horses.

As part of his movement toward Peoria, General Howard sent Lieutenant John Campbell with forty regulars up the Illinois River, where they engaged in two minor skirmishes. Troops on gunboats under Lieutenant Colonel Nicholas finally arrived at Peoria and began building a fort on September 23. The Indians under Black Partridge attempted a night attack on September 27. After approaching within one hundred and fifty yards, they were discovered. Both sides began firing at each other. Musket fire combined with grapeshot drove the attackers away, with only one soldier wounded.

Soon afterward, the rest of Howard's men arrived and moved upriver to the hostile Indian villages they found deserted. After burning the villages, the army returned to finish building the fort, which they named Fort Clark in honor of George Rogers Clark. Howard sent two other detachments further up the Illinois River. Neither one encountered any Indians. However, it was later learned that part of Major William Christ's detachment turned back just short of walking into an ambush of hundreds of warriors while searching up Bureau Creek for a Potawatomi village near present-day Tiskilwa, Illinois.

After the establishment of Fort Clark in their territory and with the defeat of the British and Indians at the Battle of the Thames, the Potawatomi lost their will to resist the Americans further. Other than a few other minor skirmishes and raids on small settlements by the various hostile tribes, and with the Kickapoo along the Embarrass River, that was the extent of fighting in Illinois in 1813. Also, William Clark, in capacity still as an Indian agent, persuaded 1500 Sauk, about a quarter of the tribe, to move west of the Mississippi River.

In January 1814, the Peoria Potawatomi met with and asked Governor Clark for peace, even leaving six warriors as hostages to guarantee good behavior. However, a few other Potawatomi warriors continued small-scale raids into Southern Illinois. As it turned out, 1814 was the bloodiest year of the entire war in Illinois.

Chapter Eleven

Prairie du Chien and Campbell's Island

Prairie du Chien

William Clark, younger brother of George Rogers Clark and of Lewis and Clark fame, became governor of the Missouri Territory in the summer of 1813. Clark, the Indian agent for the Louisiana Territory since 1807, was nominated after then-Governor Benjamin Howard resigned and took the position of military commander of the 8th district.

In early 1814, Clark learned through his spies that Robert Dickson, Britain's Indian agent in the West, was arming and stirring up the Indians against the Americans and was planning to gather a large force to attack St. Louis and Cahokia that year. Clark learned that Dickson had arrived in Prairie Du Chien, near the mouth of the Wisconsin River, with five boatloads full of goods and ammunition for the Indians.

Like other American leaders, Clark believed holding Prairie Du Chien was critical to controlling the territory and trade with the Indians. As many as 6000 Indians would yearly trade furs for essential goods at Prairie du Chien. It was Dickson's headquarters and the distribution center for trading goods. In March of 1813, Governor Ninian Edwards of Illinois Territory wrote Secretary of War William Armstrong stating, "If the British erect a fort at the mouth of the Wisconsin, and should be able to retain it two years, this, and Missouri Territory will be totally deserted; in other words conquered" Armstrong had also tentatively agreed that a fort should be built at Prairie du Chien. Therefore, on his own authority, Clark launched an expedition from St. Louis up the Mississippi River against Prairie du Chien.

Recently, Major Zachary Taylor had brought sixty-one U.S. Infantry to St. Louis. Clark utilized them for the expedition to Prairie Du Chien (Taylor had to leave for Vincennes due to family illness) and about one hundred and forty newly raised militia. He left St. Louis in five armed keelboats (gunboats) in early May. "The keelboat used in those days was a large, covered boat, or barge having a cabin extending above the deck, the sides of the cabin being far enough in from the gunwale to allow a passageway along the outside of the deck. These boats were used to carry merchandise and passengers and were propelled by poles and oars. Some had sails, and when so equipped, the bottom of the boat was supplied with a keel, from which the boats took the name keelboats."

Learning of Clark's movement, Dickson, with about three hundred Indians, vacated Prairie du Chien for Mackinac. To defend Prairie du Chien Dickson left Captain Francis Deace, a British officer, in command of a militia company with allied Sioux and Fox Indians to supplement his small force. When Clark arrived, the Indians refused to fight and fled.

Clark put his men to work building a fort named Fort Shelby in honor of the Governor of Kentucky. The fort had two blockhouses at diagonal corners with two guns, a three-pounder, and a six-pounder, mounted in one to them. Clark left Lieutenant Joseph Perkins in command with about sixty men in the fort, with the remainder on two gunboats, one named "General Clark." The "General Clark" commanded by Frederick Yeizer described as a floating blockhouse, mounted with fourteen cannons, was manned by a crew of eighty men, and was protected from musket fire.

News reached Mackinac Island on June 21 that the Americans had occupied Prairie du Chien and that they had murdered twenty Winnebago Indians. Infuriated, the Indians demanded retaliation. Lieutenant Colonel Robert Mc Douall, in command at Fort Mackinac, quickly assembled a force under Major William McKay, who led about six hundred and fifty men, of whom only one hundred and twenty were not Indians, toward Prairie du Chien. Importantly, Sergeant James Keating of the Royal Artillery and one three-pound gun were included McKay arrived at Fort Shelby on July 17. Keating's superb handling of the 3-pounder drove off the American gunboats after Captain Frederick Yeizer thought the "General Clark" would soon sink from the damage it had suffered.

Two days after the gunboats departed and after a siege of fifty-four hours, Perkins surrendered. The Americans had suffered five wounded and had lost hope that the gunboats would return. They were out of water, and with ammunition and powder nearly gone, they submitted to British terms. The British were down to their last six artillery rounds when the Americans surrendered. McKay paroled the Americans and sent them downriver to St. Louis in boats.

Campbell's Island

Meanwhile, General Howard had arrived at St Louis three days after Clark had left. Knowing the importance of holding the fort, General Howard sent reinforcements towards Prairie du Chien on July 4 in three gunboats and two sutler's barges. These gunboats were large, covered keelboats. The keelboats had a cabin extending above the deck and were propelled by poles and oars; some had sails. John Campbell commanded three gunboats of thirty-three regulars, and Lieutenants Jonathan Riggs and Stephen Rector each commanded a gunboat

Along with the regulars were sixty-six Rangers and some women and children. Undoubtedly, Governor Clark, who had returned to St Louis on June 13, must have informed General Howard that he had fired upon the Sauk at the mouth of Rock River on his way up to Prairie du Chien, but they had since sued for peace. Nevertheless, Campbell must have been somewhat wary of the unpredictable Sauk as the expedition approached the Rock River.

  When the expedition was about twenty miles below the Rock River, nine Indians in canoes approached under a white flag. The Indians had learned of the American approach and had come to meet them and lead them to their town. The Indians said that the Sauk and Fox at the village were friendly and wanted to hold a council with them. Campbell met Black Hawk at the head of one hundred and fifty warriors. Black Hawk asked Campbell if he had brought any presents for him from his father. Campbell replied that he could have the presents if he had kept his promise to Governor Clark that he would fight against the Winnebago. Black Hawk countered that he had made no promise but would fight the Winnebago if the Americans provided the necessary supplies. At the end of the parleying Campbell concluded that the Indians were friendly and rewarded them with a gift of whiskey. The following is the account of the Battle of Campbells Island as written by William Meese.

  On the morning of July 19, before breakfast, the boats all set sail and started up the river, with a fine breeze. During the night a party of Indians arrived at the Sac village from Prairie du Chien, coming down Rock river bringing the Sacs six kegs of powder and telling them that the fort at Prairie du Chien had been captured by the British. These messengers told the Sacs (Sauks) that the British wished them again to join them in the war against the Americans, which the Indians agreed to do.

Black Hawk's memory is at fault, he does not state exactly what these Indian messengers told him. Colonel McKay, whose army of British and Indians had attacked Prairie du Chien, in a letter to his superior officer, under date of July 27, 1814, says that on the seventeenth of July about three o'clock in the afternoon, after the gun boat "Governor Clark" had been driven from its position by the British cannon and had started down the river, that he immediately sent off a canoe with three men, an Iowan, who had come from Mackinac with him, and two of the six Sauks, who had joined him on the Fox river, that he gave them four kegs of gun powder and ordered them to pass the "Governor Clark" and get as soon as possible to the Rapids at the Rock river, where he believed the gun boat would run aground; that they should collect all the Sauks and annoy the "Governor Clark" and prevent their landing to get fire wood, etc.

Black Hawk collected his warriors and determined to attack the boats which had now started up the river, as Black Hawk says: "I collected my warriors and determined to pursue the boats, I immediately started with my party by land, in pursuit, thinking that some of their boats might get aground, or that the GREAT SPIRIT would put them in our power, if he wished them taken."

The boats had just passed the head of Rock Island, when the boat commanded by Major Campbell was grounded on the rocks, and he was compelled to discharge and put off part of her loading into the other boats before he could release his boat.

After proceeding about six miles the wind increased to a hurricane. Campbell's boat being still heavily loaded he says: "I was afraid of her dashing to pieces on the rocks, and ordered her to be put to shore, which in doing from severe gale of wind which was blowing, and the roughness of the water dashed her so hard on the shore it was impossible to get her off while the storm lasted." The boat was driven on the north shore of an island lying about six miles east of Moline and which since that day has been known as Campbell's Island. It lies near the eastern shore and belongs to the state of Illinois.

Black Hawk says, "About half way up the rapids I had a full view of the boats, all sailing with a strong wind, I soon discovered one boat badly managed and was suffered to be driven ashore, by the wind, they landed by running hard aground, and lowered their sail, the others passed on."

The ground where the boat landed was covered with high grass, hazel and willow bushes for a considerable distance up and down the shore. Campbell immediately placed two sentinels about sixty yards from the boats, and the men commenced getting their breakfast.

They had not been on the Island more than twenty-five or thirty minutes when the Indians commenced their attack, both sentinels were killed the first fire, and one other man on shore. Campbell ordered the cable cut and the boat to be gotten off, in doing of which two men were killed and three wounded. Finding the gale blowed directly on land, and that it was impossible to get her off he ordered his men to defend the boat to the last extremity.

The boats of Lieutenants Rector and Riggs were about three miles up the river at this time, Lieutenant Riggs' boat being in advance he heard the report of the firing and saw the smoke rising from where Campbell's boat lay, he tacked his boat and signaled Rector, who tacked his boat and both sailed for Campbell's boat. Rector's boat being the first to reach the scene of the battle. Savages were seen among the trees and bushes, and a large number of Indians were seen coming in canoes from the eastern shore. It was estimated that about four hundred Indians surrounded them. The savages commenced giving their war-whoop and pouring in on them a fire of musketry and arrows. Major Campbell's right wrist was fractured by a musket ball during the first onslaught, and he was carried into the cabin of his boat and laid on a bunk, while his men gallantly returned the fire of the Indians.

Campbell's boat was so near the bank that the Indians were able to fire in at the port oar holes. The storm had now become so violent that it was fully an hour before the other boats were able to come to Campbell's assistance.

Riggs' boat was driven ashore about one hundred yards below Campbell's boat, and Rector to avoid a similar fate, had let go an anchor, and lay about twenty yards above Campbell's boat, the rangers from both barges kept up a brisk fire on the Indians.

This unequal contest waged for several hours, when the firing from Campbell's boat becoming less frequent, led Lieutenant Rector to believe that most of Campbell's men were either killed or wounded.

Riggs' boat was the best fortified, but his crew had been weakened. When Campbell's boat was stranded on the rocks he sent a sergeant and ten men to help him off and Campbell did not return the men.

Rector's boat had among its crew many of the French from Cahokia who were experienced sailors. The wind was still a raging tempest, and the fire of the Indians was becoming more destructive to the boats; at this time Black Hawk says: "I prepared by bow and arrows to throw fire to the sail, which was laying on the boat, and after two or three attempts succeeded in setting the sail on fire." Campbell's boat was soon in flames. Lieutenant Rector could not remain inactive and witness the horrible death of Campbell and his companions. In the face of the tempest and the galling fire of the foe, he cut his anchors, a number of his men got out into the water, keeping the boat between them and the Indians, they pushed their boat against the fire of the Indians up to Campbell's boat, and then those who were unhurt; so loaded was Rector's boat that the water was running in at the oar holes and almost all of their provisions were thrown overboard to lighten the boat. The Indians all the time kept up a murderous fire. In taking the men from Campbell's boat the Major was shot through the body. Black Hawk in his autobiography states at this time: "We wounded the war chief."

Rector's men still in the water, and keeping the boat between them and the Indians, hauled their boat out into the stream, swimming alongside of the boat until the channel was reached and the boat had been carried out of gunshot, when they climbed into the boat.

Rector's boat was crowded, but the men took to their oars and rowed night and day until they reached St. Louis. The casualties on all the boats totaled thirty-seven, sixteen killed and twenty-one wounded. According to Meese. "Rector and his men risked their lives to save their comrades, and the battle at Campbell's Island has no equal for daring and heroism during the War of 1812 in the West."

Lieutenant John Weaver of the Regulars, who was second in command on Campbell's boat, acted bravely; primarily by his exertions, the wounded were safely transferred to Rector's boat.

Almost all the ammunition for the expedition and the supplies for Fort Shelby, except a box of musket balls, was on Campbell's boat and was captured by Black Hawk; nothing was saved. The Regulars fought with their shirts off, keeping only their arms and fatigue overalls.

The gunboat "Governor Clark," which had fled Prairie du Chien two days before, arrived in the afternoon at the end of the battle. Yeizer in the "Governor Clark" had first encountered the two unarmed sutler's barges of Campbell's expedition and saw Riggs still fighting the Indians but was too distant to be of assistance. Yeizer anchored the gunboat for the night before escorting the two unarmed barges past Campbell's grounded burnt gunboat the next morning.

At the gunboat site, Black Hawk stated that they had put out the fire on the boat to save the remainder of the cargo. He poured out the whiskey from several barrels and distributed several guns and some clothing to his braves. He and his warriors later celebrated at their village by dancing over the scalps they had taken in the battle.

Black Hawk later claimed that the Indians only suffered two casualties, but based on the intensity and length of the battle, this was undoubtedly higher.

Chapter Twelve

Credit Island

When General Howard learned of the defeat of Campbell's expedition, he immediately prepared for a retaliatory strike on the now-hostile Sauk village. Howard now ordered twenty-nine-year-old Major Zachary Taylor to lead an expedition against the Sauk. Taylor was to try to row his gunboats up the Rock River and bombard Saukenuk from the river. If possible, to do so safely, he was also to destroy the Indian cornfields. When done, he was to proceed back down the Mississippi and build a fort opposite the mouth of the Des Moines River.

Meanwhile, the new commander at Fort Mc Kay (Prairie du Chien), Captain Thomas Anderson, received news of Taylor's expedition. British Lieutenant Duncan Graham had come to him with a Sauk request for men and guns to help them repel Taylor's expected attack. Before this, Anderson had discounted a Sauk report of the American expedition in order to gain additional supplies for themselves. Knowing that if he failed to send aid to the Indians, he risked losing their support, Anderson sent Graham to the Rock River with a detachment of thirty men, including the artillerist Sargent Keating, a three-pounder, and two swivel guns. Graham would write to him, stating, "Our coming here has given more satisfaction to the Sauks than if all the goods in the King's store in Mackinac has been sent them, as they are now firmly convinced that their English Father is determined to support them against the ambition and unjust conduct of their enemies."

On August 23, Taylor left Cap Au Gris, a small French hamlet near the mouth of the Illinois River, in eight large fortified keelboats, with a detachment of three hundred and thirty-four men, of whom forty were regulars. To fool the Indians into thinking the object of the expedition was Prairie du Chien, Taylor's force passed north of the mouth of the Rock River, where they saw many Indians. The wind began to blow with hurricane force and blew Taylor's boats toward the tiny island above Credit Island, where Taylor landed about four o'clock in the afternoon on September 4th. During the night, Indians landed on the Island, approached Taylor's sentries undetected, and suddenly began to fire on Taylor's men.

Major Zachary Taylor's account of the battle is as follows:

"On my arrival at the mouth of Rock River, the Indians began to make their appearance in considerable numbers; running up the Mississippi to the upper village and crossing the river below us. After passing Rock River, which is very small at the mouth, from an attentive and careful examination, as I proceeded up the Mississippi, I was confident it was impossible for us to enter its mouth with our large boats. Immediately opposite its most large island commences, which together with the western shore of the Mississippi, was covered with a considerable number of horses, which were doubtless placed in those situations in order to draw small detachments on shore; but in this they were disappointed, and I determined to alter the plan which you had suggested, which was to pass the different villages as if the object of the expedition was Prairie du Chien, for several reasons. First, that I might have an opportunity of viewing the situation of the ground to enable me to select such a landing as would bring our artillery to bear on the villages with the greatest advantage. I was likewise in hopes a party would approach us with a flag, from which I expected to learn the situation of affairs, at the Prairie, and ascertain in some measure their numbers and perhaps bring them to a council, which I should have been able to have retaliated on them for their repeated acts of treachery; or, if they were determined to attack draw them some distance from their towns towards the rapids, run down in the night and destroy them before they could return to their defense. But in this I was disappointed. The wind, which had been in our favor, began to shift about at the time we passed the mouth of Rock River, and by the time we reached the head of the island, which is about a mile and a half long, it blew a perfect hurricane, quarterly down the river, and it was with great difficulty we made land on a small island, containing six or eight acres, covered with willows, near the middle of the river, and about sixty yards from the upper end of the island. In this situation I determined to remain during the night if the storm continued, as I knew the anchors of several of the boats in that event would not hold them, and there was a great probability of their being drifted on sandbars, of which the river is full in this place, which would have exposed the men very much in getting them off, even if they could have prevented their filling with water.

"It was about 4 o'clock in the evening when we were compelled to land, and large parties of Indians were on each side of the river, as well as crossing in different directions in canoes; but no gun was fired from either side. The wind continued to blow the whole night with violence, accompanied with some rain, which induced me to order the sentinels to be brought in placed in the bow of each boat. About daylight, Captain Whiteside's boat was fired on at the distance of about fifteen paces, and a corporal, who was on the outside of the boat, was mortally wounded. My orders were, if a boat was fired on, to return it, but not a man to leave the boat without positive orders from myself. So soon as it got perfectly light, as the enemy continued about the boat, I determined to drive their numbers be what they might, provided we were able to do so. I then assigned each boat a proper guard, formed the troops for action and pushed through the willows to the opposite shore; but those fellows who had the boldness to fire on the boats cleared themselves as soon as the troops were formed by wading from the island we were encamped on to the one just below us. Captain Whiteside, who was on the left, was able to give them a warm fire as they reached the island they had retreated to. They returned the fire for a few moments, then they retreated. In this affair we had two men badly wounded. When Captain Whiteside commenced the fire, I ordered Captain Rector (different Rector than Campbell fight) to drop down with his boat to ground and to rake the island below with artillery, and to fire on every canoe he should discover passing from one shore to the other, which should come within reach. In this situation he remained about one hour, and no Indians making their appearance, he determined to drop down the island sixty yards, and destroy several canoes that were lying to shore. This he effected, and just on setting his men on board, the British commenced a fire on our boats with a six, a four and two swivels, from behind a knoll that completely covered them. The boats were entirely exposed to the artillery, which was distant three hundred and fifty paces from us. So soon as the first gun fired, I ordered a six-pounder to be brought out and placed, but on recollecting a moment, I found the boat would be sunk before any impression could be made on them by our cannon, as they were completely under cover, and had already brought their guns to bear on our boats, for the round shot from their six passed through Lieutenant Hempstead's boat and shattered her considerably. I then ordered the boats to drop down, which was done in order, and conducted with the greatest coolness by every officer, although exposed to a constant fire from their artillery for more than half a mile.

So soon as they commenced firing from their artillery, the Indians raised a yell and commenced firing on us from every direction, whether they were able to do us any danger or not. From each side of the river, Captain Rector, who was laying to the shore of the island, was attacked the instant the first gun was fired, by a very large party, and in a close and well contested action of about fifteen minutes, they drove them, after giving three rounds of grape from his three-pounder.

Captain Whiteside, who was nearest to Captain Rector, dropped down and anchored nigh him, and gave the enemy several fires with his swivel; but the wind was so hard down stream as to drift his anchor. Captain Rector, at that moment, got his boat off, and we were then exposed to the fire of the Indians for two miles, which we returned with interest from our set of artillery whenever we could get them to bear. I was compelled to drop down about three miles before a proper place presented itself for landing, as but few of the boats had anchors sufficient to stop them in the river. Here I halted for the purpose of having the wounded attended and some of the boats repaired, as some of them had been injured by the enemy's artillery. They followed us in their boats until we halted on a small prairie and prepared for action, when they returned in as great hurry as they followed us.

I then collected the officers together and put the following question to them: "Are we able, three hundred and thirty-four effective men, officers, non-commissioned officers and privates, to fight the enemy with any prospect of success and effect, which is to destroy their villages and corn?" They were of the opinion the enemy was at least three men to one, and that it was not practicable to effect either object. I then determined to drop down the river to the Lemoine without delay, as some of the ranging officers informed me their men were short of provisions, and execute the principal object of the expedition, in erecting a fort to command the river. This shall be effected as soon as practicable with the means in my power, and should the enemy attempt to descend the river in force before the fort can be completed, every foot of the way from the fort to the settlement shall be contested

"In the affair at Rock River, I had eleven men badly wounded, three mortally, of whom one has since died. I am much indebted to the officers for their prompt obedience to orders, nor do I believe a braver set of men could have been collected than those who compose this detachment. But, sir I conceive it would have been madness in me, as well as a direct violation of my orders, to have risked the detachment without a prospect of success. I believe I should have been fully able to have accomplished your views if the enemy had not been supplied with artillery and so advantageously posted as to render it impossible for us to have dislodged him without imminent danger, of the loss of the whole detachment.

The British artillery had been the primary factor in Taylor's defeat. Writing the day after the battle, Graham said that of the fifty-four shots fired at the boats, only three or four did not go through them. In addition, Graham said that if they had a greater supply of ammunition and provisions, they could have pursued Taylor as far as the Rapids of the Des Moines River. He again gave credit to the skill and courage of Sergeant Keating.

Taylor's repulse at the Rock River would be the only time in his life that he ever retreated in the midst of battle, and he considered it a blemish on his record In the aftermath of the fighting, Taylor descended the Mississippi River about one hundred miles and built Fort Johnson opposite the mouth of the Des Moines River. While the fort was being built, work parties were under continual harassment by the Indians. Because of the failure of supplies to get through due to an Indian attack on a provision boat, Taylor was forced to burn the fort and return to Cap au Gris.

Credit Island received its name because both Indians and fur traders would receive credit for supplies at the trading post there in the early 1800s before they set out for their winter trapping. When they returned in the spring, they would settle their accounts.

Chapter Thirteen

Between Wars

The Treaty of Ghent was signed in December 1814 and ratified on February 7, 1815. Officially, it marked the end of the War of 1812. Unfortunately, news of the treaty spread slowly and did not reach Illinois until the first week of March, Mackinac Island until May, and Prairie du Chien until May 22. During the winter, Captain AM. Bulger at Fort McKay appealed to the various tribes to keep fighting. He announced that the King was faithful to them and would not sign a treaty with the Americans until the boundaries were restored to those before the Treaty of Greenville. He also told them that additional reinforcements were forthcoming. Therefore, the Indians ignored peace rumors originating from St. Louis, and in February and March, they continued to raid and murder settlers along the Ohio and Wabash Rivers.

Within only a few days of Bulger's speech encouraging continuing Indian support of the British, the situation changed dramatically. After Bulger learned of the Peace Treaty, the British held a conference with the Indians of the Northwest Territory in June of 1815, informing them of the news and admonishing them to make peace with the Americans. The British told the Indians that the treaty guaranteed "all the possessions, rights and privileges they may have enjoyed, or been entitled to in 1811 provided they ceased hostilities against the United States." If the Indians did not halt their hostilities, they would lose the benefits the British had negotiated for them. As a further signal to the tribes that the British would no longer support hostilities toward the Americans, they vacated and burned

Fort Mc Cay at Prairie du Chien in May.

Before news of peace had reached the Sauk, war chief Black Hawk had led a war party to Fort Howard at the mouth of the Cuivre River in Missouri. Thus, Black Hawk would fight the last battle of the War of 1812 on May 24, 1815. Upon arrival, Black Hawk's warriors ambushed a detachment of five men in sight of the fort, killing four.

Captain Peter Craig's Rangers immediately left the fort and attacked the war party holed up in a giant sinkhole.

The following is Black Hawk's account of the fight, as stated in his autobiography.

> The enemy rushed upon us without giving us time to reload. They surrounded us, and forced us to run into a deep sink-hole, at the bottom of which there were some bushes. We loaded our guns, and awaited the approach of the enemy. They rushed to the edge of the hole and fired, killing one of our men.
>
> We returned the fire instantly, and killed one of their party! We reloaded, and commenced digging holes in the side of the bank to protect ourselves, whilst a party watched the movements of the enemy, expecting that their whole force would be upon us immediately. Some of my warriors commenced singing their death-songs! I heard the whites talking-and called to them, "'to come out and fight!" I did not like my situation, and wished the matter settled. I soon heard chopping and knocking. I could not imagine what they were doing. Soon after they run up wheels with a battery on it, and fired down without hurting any of us. I called to them again, and told them if they were "brave men, to come down and fight us." They gave up the siege, and returned to their fort about dusk.

There were eighteen in this trap with me. We all got out safe and found one white man dead on the edge of the sink-hole. They did not remove him, for fear of our fire. We scalped him, and placed our dead man upon him! We could not have left him in a better situation, than on an enemy!

In July, American peace commissioners, governors Clark and Edwards, and Auguste Chouteau met with most of the tribes at Portage des Sioux in Missouri Territory just north of St. Louis. The commissioners signed a formal peace treaty with the Potawatomi of the Illinois River and the Piankashaw. They agreed to recognize all land cessions made between 1795 and 1811 and to cease their relations with the British. The remainder of the Potawatomi resisted, stating that they had lived on the Illinois River for the past fifty years. Therefore, the 1804 treaty with the Sauk and Fox did not include or apply to them. When surveyors came to their lands, the Potawatomi threatened to kill them and destroy their equipment. Finally, the following year, at a council in St. Louis, they acceded to American demands and agreed to sell land they occupied for the first time. They ceded all their land west from the southern tip of Lake Michigan with the condition they could use for hunting until Americans occupied it. The Potawatomi would almost continuously make land cessions from 1818 until 1833, when they sold the last of their land in Illinois. Altogether, they negotiated twenty-eight treaties in those years, yielding eighteen million acres to the United States.

Almost immediately after the end of the war, Americans were surveying the land between the Illinois and Mississippi Rivers. As early as the winter of 1815-1816, Chief Little Otter of the Kickapoo responded by sending war belts to the Potawatomi, Miami, and other Indians to resist the American intrusions on their lands. However, all the tribes refused to join in what they perceived as a futile resistance. In 1816, the U.S.

commenced negotiations with the various tribes of the Northwest Territory to extinguish their land titles and to resettle the tribes west of the Mississippi River. Between 1816 and 1818, Peoria, the Kaskaskia, and other small tribes ceded their remaining lands to the U.S., freeing southern and western Illinois for settlement.

Yet the Kickapoo, still not resigned to American domination, stole horses from settlers and burned dwellings. They also harassed surveyors by damaging surveying equipment and pulling up field stakes. The United States reacted by sending out patrols of rangers and furnished troops to guard the surveyors. Finally, under continued American pressure to relocate in 1819, both the Illinois and Wabash bands of the Kickapoo signed the treaties. They agreed to move to land on the Osage River in Missouri. Though about 2000 Kickapoo moved to Missouri in September, two bands of about two hundred and fifty Kickapoo remained and continued to cause trouble stealing from and harassing settlers. It was not until 1835 that the final two small bands of Kickapoo migrated west of the Mississippi. Meanwhile, Black Hawk of the Sauk tribe attracted about one hundred Kickapoo warriors and their families under the Kickapoo war chief: Panoahah, to join them at their settlement on the Rock River.

After 1815, settlers began to flood into Illinois territory, still under the governance of Ninian Edwards (territorial governor from 1809 to 1818). Rapidly, territorial politicians began to push for statehood. The Northwest Ordinance of 1787 required the territorial population to be at least 60,000 for admittance as a state. A census showed the population to be 40,258 in August of 1818. While the bill for statehood was moving through Congress, Nathaniel Pope introduced an amendment moving the state's boundary from a point ten miles north of the tip of Lake Michigan to a point forty-one miles further north, thus adding 8000 square miles to Illinois. Allowing an exception to the population requirement for statehood,

President James Monroe signed an act making Illinois the twenty-first state in the union on December 3, 1818. Shadrach Bond became the first governor and moved the capital from Kaskaskia to Vandalia.

No peace treaty had been signed in 1815 with the Sauk, who had largely avoided the peace conference at Portage des Sioux in 1815. They had killed the messenger sent to summon them to the treaty. In another hostile act, Black Hawk led thirty warriors to revenge the killing of a young Sauk hunter by Illinois volunteers in Southern Illinois. His war party killed seven Illinois Volunteers about thirty miles northwest of St. Louis. Because of acts like this, Andrew Jackson advocated for a military expedition against the Sauk. Finally, the Sauk met in an acrimonious conference with Clark in St. Louis and signed a treaty in May 1816. In the treaty, the Sauk agreed to recognize the terms of the 1804 treaty in which they had decided to relinquish their lands in Illinois. Black Hawk also signed the treaty. However, the Sauk later said that they were never told the terms of the first article, which required them to cede their lands above the Rock River. After the treaty, the Sauk living in Missouri began to separate themselves from the "Rock River" Sauk, who never forgave them for affirming the 1804 treaty.

When the treaty was being negotiated, a U.S. infantry regiment under Colonel George Davenport and about seven hundred fifty soldiers and laborers arrived at Rock Island. They started building Fort Armstrong, which was not far from the village of Saukenuk. This was part of an overall policy to keep the peace between the various tribes. New forts were also constructed at other strategic locations. The army built Fort Crawford at Prairie du Chien, Fort Howard at Green Bay, and rebuilt Fort Dearborn in Chicago. They chose the location at Rock Island to keep a careful watch over the Sauk and Fox. Black Hawk stated that when he saw the fort under construction on his return home, he believed it contradicted the spirit of the peace treaty. Instead, he thought that the U.S. government was preparing for war in a time of peace. Black Hawk stated that the Indians were very sorry to lose the use of Rock Island. He called it the best Island on the Mississippi as it supplied the Indians with abundant varieties of berries, fruits, and nuts. The war was over, but the seeds for the next war had already been planted, and Black Hawk would lead the fight.

Nevertheless, for the present, settlers did not yet covet the land where the Sauk hunted, fished, and farmed, and the Indians were allowed to live there in peace. In the years preceding the Black Hawk War, the Sauk prospered. The British still supplied the Sauk with trade goods when they made their yearly journey to Fort Malden or Drummond Island, forty-five miles northeast of Mackinac. In 1819, the British agent at the fort distributed $3400 worth of goods to the thousands of Sauk who made the journey. The Sauk still hunted successfully for fur, enabling them to trade for their needed supplies. In 1818-1819, the Sauk sold 60,082 assorted raccoon, muskrat, deerskins, and a combined 5000 pelts of beaver, bear, otter, mink, and lynx. The Sauk (primarily women) earned additional income from mining lead. Major Marsten said they mined lead, which totaled four or five thousand pounds in a year.

During this interwar period, the Sauk were strong and growing stronger. In 1818, the Indian agent Thomas Forsyth estimated the Sauk could field 1000 well-armed warriors with good rifles. By 1826, he said they could muster 1200 warriors out of a little less than 5000 population. During this period, the Sauk expended their strength by fighting only against other Indians. They fought against Otos and Osages in Missouri, and especially against the Sioux, whom they battled almost every summer. In one large-scale expedition to take scalps in 1822, the Sauk combined with the Fox and Iowa tribes to the number of five hundred in an invasion of Sioux territory. Part of the reason for these internal conflicts was the increasing scarcity of game. By 1824, the Sauk began to travel two hundred to three hundred miles to achieve success in hunting game. However, soon, the Sauk would forget any conflicts with other Indians as increasing American intrusion on their land became the focus of all their attention.

Before the Sauk engaged in conflict with the Americans, another tribe's festering resentment of the Americans would erupt into hostilities. On June 28, 1827, a small band of Winnebago started a short-lived conflict in Southern Wisconsin, labeled the Winnebago War. It is mentioned here because, after the war, the Winnebago tribe (primarily residing in Wisconsin) ceded their land north of the Rock River in Illinois.

The Winnebago were already simmering with hostility toward the Americans because many miners had intruded onto their claimed mining lands in Northern Illinois. Thousands of miners were presently occupying their lands. In the Fever River (now Galena River) region around Galena, Illinois, the population of miners expanded from five hundred and forty in December of 1825 to perhaps 1000-1500 by the end of 1826. The miners cut into the income of the Winnebago, who had used their proceeds from mining to purchase trade goods.

This already hostile atmosphere was further inflamed when a group of Winnebago murdered members of a Metis family near Prairie du Chien. The Winnebago surrendered two men, Wau-koo-kau and Man-ne-tah-peh-keh. The two prisoners were moved to Fort Snelling when the garrison abandoned Fort Crawford in the summer of 1826. In response, some Winnebago sent war pipes to the Santee Sioux. Finally, violence erupted when the rumor spread that the two Winnebago warriors held in custody at Fort Crawford had been executed. A warrior named Red Bird and some companions entered the farmhouse of Rigeste Gagnier near Prairie de Chien and murdered him, an infant child and a hired hand. Shortly afterward, they joined the rest of their band at the mouth of the Bad Axe River. Red Bird's band enjoyed a few days of alcohol-fueled revelry there, including a celebratory scalp dance. Meanwhile, one of several keelboats owned by Mr. Lindsay on its return from dropping off provisions at Fort Snelling approached the Winnebago encampment.

What happened next was the only battle of the Winnebago War by Wm. J. Snelling as recorded in the *History of Crawford and Richland Counties, Wisconsin.*

> So strong was the wind that all the force of the sweeps could scarcely stem it, and by the time the foremost boat was near the encampment, at the mouth of the Bad Ax, the crew were very willing to stop and rest. One or two Frenchmen, or half-breeds, who were on board observed hostile appearances on shore, and advised the rest to keep the middle of the stream with the boat, but their council was disregarded. Most of the crew were Americans, who, as usual with our countrymen, combined a profound ignorance of Indian character with a thorough contempt for Indian prowess. They urged the boat directly toward the camp with all the force of the sweeps. There were sixteen men on deck.
>
> The men were rallying their French companions on their apprehensions, as the boat approached the shore; but when within thirty yards of the bank, suddenly the trees and rocks rang with the blood-chilling, ear-piercing tones of the war-whoop, and a volley of rifle balls rained upon the deck. Happily, the Winnebagoes had not yet recovered from the effects of their debauch, and their arms were not steady. One man only fell. He was a little negro named Peter. His leg was

dreadfully shattered and he afterward died of the wound... All this passed in as little time as it will take to read this paragraph... Presently a voice hailed the boat in the Sac tongue demanding to know if the crew were English? A half-free Sac, named Beauchamp, answered in the affirmative. "then," said the querist, "come on shore, and we will do you no harm, for we are your brethren, the sacs." "Dog," retorted Beauchamp, "no Sac would attack us thus cowardly. If you want us on shore, you must come and fetch us."

With that, a second volley soon came from the shore; but, as the men were lying prone in the bottom of the boat, below the water line, they all escaped but one. One man, an American named Stewart, fell. He had risen to return the first fire, and muzzle of his musket protruding through a loop-hole, showed some Winnebago where to aim. The bullet struck him under the left arm, and passed directly through his heart. He fell dead, with his finger on the trigger of his undischarged gun. It was a hot day, and before the fight was over, the scent of gunpowder could not overpower the stench of the red puddle around him.

The Winnebagoes encouraged by the non-resistance, now rushed to their canoes, with intent to board. One venerable old man endeavored to dissuade them. He laid hold on one of the canoes, and would, perhaps, have succeeded in retaining it; but in the heat of his argument, a ball from the boat hit him in the middle finger of the peace-making hand. Very naturally enraged at such unkind treatment from his friends, he loosed the canoe, hurried to his wigwam for his gun, and took an active part in the remainder of the action. In the meanwhile, the white men had recovered from their first panic, and seized their arms. The boarders were received with a very severe discharge. In one canoe two savages were killed with the same bullet. Their dying struggles upset the canoe, and the rest were obliged to swim on shore, where it was sometime before they could restore their arms to fighting order. Several more were wounded, and those who remained unhurt, put back, satisfied that a storm was not the best mode of attack.

Two, however, persevered. They were together in one canoe, and approached the boat astern, where there were no holes through which the whites could fire upon them. They soon leaped on board. One seized the long steering oar, or rudder. The other jumped upon deck, where he halted, and discharged five muskets, which had been left by the crew, fled below through the deck into the bottom of the boat. In this manner he wounded one man very severely. After this exploit, he hurried to the bow, where he seized a long pole, and with the assistance of the steersman, succeeded in grounding the boat on a sand-bar, and fixing her fast under the fire of his people. The two Winnebago boatmen then began to load and fire, to the no small annoyance of the crew. He at the stern was soon dispatched. One of the whites observed his position through a crack, and gave him a mortal wound through the boards. Still, he struggled to get overboard, probably to save his scalp. But his struggles were feeble, and a second bullet terminated them before he could effect his object. After the fight was over, the man who slew him took his scalp.

The bow of the boat was open, and the warrior there still kept his station, out of sight, excepting when he stooped to fire, which he did five times. His third shot broke the arm, and passed through the lungs, of the brave Beauchamp. At this sight, one or two began to speak of surrender. "No, friends," cried the dying man; "you will not save your lives so. Fight to the last; for they will show no mercy. If they get the better of you, for God's sake throw me overboard. Do not let them get my hair." He continued to exhort them to resistance long as his breath lasted, and died with the words "fight on" on his lips. Before this time, however, his slayer had also taken his leave of life. A sailor, named Jack Mandeville, shot him through the head, and he fell overboard, carrying his gun with him.

From that moment Mandeville assumed the command of the boat. A few had resolved to take the skiff, and leave the rest to their fate. They had already cast off the rope. Jack interposed, declaring that he would shoot the first man, and bayonet the second, who would persevere. They submitted. Two more had hidden themselves in the bow of the boat, out of sight, but not out of danger. After a while the old tar missed them, sought them, and compelled them by threats of instant death, enforced by pricks of his bayonet, to leave their hiding place, and take share in the business in hand. Afterwards they fought like bull dogs. It was well for them that Mandeville acted as he did; for they had scarcely risen when a score of bullets at least, passed through the place where they had been lying.

After the two or three first volleys the fire had slackened, but it was not, therefore, the less dangerous. The Indians had the advantage of superior numbers, and could shift their positions at pleasure. The whites were compelled to lie in the bottom of the boat, below the water mark, for its sides were without bulwarks. Every bullet passed through and through. It was only at intervals, and very warily, that they could rise to fire; for the flash of every gun showed the position of the marksman, and was instantly followed by the reports of two or three Indian rifles. On the other hand they were not seen, and being thinly scattered over a large boat, the Winnebagoes could but guess their positions. The fire, was therefore, slow; for none on either side cared to waste ammunition. Thus, for upwards of three hours, the boatmen lay in blood and bilge-water, deprived of the free use of their limbs, and wholly unable to extricate themselves.

At last, as the night fell, Mandeville came to the conclusion that darkness would render the guns of his own party wholly useless, while it would not render the aim of the Winnebagoes a lot less certain. He, therefore, as soon as it was dark, stoutly called for assistance, and sprang into the water. Four more followed him. The balls rained around them, passing through their clothes; but they persisted, and the boat was soon afloat. Seeing their prey escaping, the Winnebagoes raised a yell of mingled rage and despair, and gave the whites a farewell volley. It was returned, with three hearty cheers, and ere a gun could be re-loaded, the boat had floated out of shooting distance...

Thirty-seven Indians were engaged in this battle, seven of whom were killed, and fourteen were wounded. They managed to put 693 balls into and through the boat. Two of the crew were killed outright, two mortally, and two slightly wounded. Jack Mandeville's courage and presence of mind undoubtedly saved the rest, as well as the boat; but we have never heard that he was rewarded in any way or shape.

Mr. Lindsay's boat, the rear one, reached the mouth of the Bad Ax about midnight. The Indians opened a fire upon her, which was promptly returned. There was a light on board, at which the first gun was probably aimed, for that bill only hit the boat. All the rest passed over harmless in the darkness.

In early September, Major Whistler from Fort Howard at Green Bay and General Henry Atkinson converged on the hostile Winnebago near the Wisconsin and Fox Rivers portage. Whistler arrived first and demanded the surrender of the murderers. The Winnebago gave up Red Bird immediately and six others three weeks later. Red Bird and two others were imprisoned and sentenced to death.

Warriors from several other tribes used the Winnebago uprising as an excuse to commit their own depredations. Fearing the threat of a Potawatomi attack on Chicago, one trader hurried to Danville, Illinois, to recruit a militia force of one hundred men to defend the growing village. The Santee Sioux chief, Wabasha, prevented further bloodshed when he held back his warriors from joining the uprising.

A delegation of Winnebago traveled to Washington in the spring of 1828 to seek a pardon for their fellow tribesman on the condition that the Winnebago ceded their land above the Rock River in Illinois and land in Southern Wisconsin. President John Quincy Adams agreed. In a treaty signed at Prairie du Chien in 1829, the Winnebago gave up their land for an annual payment of $18,000. Simultaneously, the Three Fires or Confederation of (Potawatomi, Ottawa, and Chippewa relinquished their claims in the same region for an annual remittance of $18,000.

Though a minor war, The Winnebago War had far-reaching and life-changing consequences for the Winnebago and other Indians. To strengthen the military presence in the region and thereby awe the tribes into submission, the United States re-garrisoned Fort Crawford and Fort Dearborn. Also, Fort Winnebago was built by the Fox-Wisconsin River portage and was garrisoned by one hundred and ten soldiers.

Before the war, most Americans believed the argument that the Indians could be assimilated and civilized. President John Q. Adams reflected a reversal in opinion when, in the State of the Union address, he said that the civilization policy was a failure and that future policy should require the removal of the tribes west of the Mississippi River. The government would soon act on this policy regarding the Sauk.

There had been almost constant inter-tribal conflicts between the various tribes of the upper Midwest region, including Illinois, during the entire period between the War of 1812 and the Black Hawk War. One such conflict just before the war would have a minor impact. In the summer of 1830, a party of Santee Sioux and Menominee killed fifteen of sixteen Fox delegates invited to a meeting in the Fever River Region by the Fox subagent. The following summer, about one hundred Sauk and Fox warriors retaliated by massacring twenty-six Menominee at Prairie du Chien. The Santee Sioux and the Menominee would assist the Americans in apprehending the Sauk and Fox during the Black Hawk War.

Summary Part III War of 1812 Period

The Americans enjoyed very little success in Illinois during the War of 1812. They were massacred at Fort Dearborn, forced to abandon Fort Madison (In Iowa, but attacked by Indians from Illinois), and defeated by the Sauk and Fox at the battles of Campbell's Island and Credit Island. The Americans achieved their only real success around Peoria, driving the Potawatomi and others away.

Despite losing battles in Illinois, the Americans succeeded in the peace negotiations. They drove the British, other than a few traders, out of the Northwest Territory. The British would never again ally themselves with the Indians in another war with the United States. Knowing they had no backing from the British, most of the Indians in Illinois reluctantly accepted peace terms. They ceded land to the Americans in return for annuities after a few years of minor resistance.

The Sauk and Fox were the exception. They had won victories over the Americans during the war and remained undefeated. Most of the Sauk eventually moved west across the Mississippi in the ensuing years. However, a minority of the tribe remained influenced by the British when they trekked each year to Fort Malden for British trade goods and gifts. Unfortunately, this so-called "British Band" held out the misguided hope that the British would still assist them in any future conflict. This belief would lead to disastrous results when they struggled to keep their homeland under Black Hawk. This struggle would lead to war when the government of the recently established state of Illinois (1818) decided to remove the remaining Sauk and Fox as land-hungry Americans began to settle around Saukenuk in the late 1820s.

Part IV
The Black Hawk War

Chapter Fourteen

Prelude to War

Signing treaties in 1816 and 1825, the Sauk seemed to accede to the terms of the Treaty of 1804. They never physically resisted its enforcement. However, it is highly doubtful they understood its full implications. They probably believed they would continue to use the land as they had in the past, though the United States claimed political sovereignty. They had experienced something similar with the French and the British, where nothing had changed. They definitely would not have knowingly sold their villages and best hunting grounds, and they always insisted that they had not sold any land north of the Rock River in Illinois.

Black Hawk later stated that he did not understand that the Sauk would have to give up their village, Saukenuk, on the Rock River. The Sauk had driven the Kaskaskia from the Saukenuk area and had settled there at least a decade before the American Revolution after migrating from Wisconsin. When the French arrived, they had lived near Montreal but had been driven east by the Iroquois and then the Ojibwa. Explorer Jonathan Carver described Saukenuk as "the largest and best-built town" he had ever seen. The town was laid out in straight, wide streets bordered by ninety multi-family lodges. Black Hawk reputedly was born in Saukenuk, the largest of all the Sauk towns, in 1767. Black Hawk had a passionate devotion to his home there. He would never have signed a treaty that required giving it up. He said that what he and his nation knew of the delegation and the treaty details were as follows:

> The American chief told them he wanted land, and they agreed to give him some on the west side of the Mississippi and some on the Illinois side, opposite the Jefferson. When the business was all arranged, they expected to have their friend released to come home with them. But about the time they were ready to start, their friend was let out of prison, who ran a short distance and was shot dead. This was all they could recollect of what was said and done. They had been drunk most of the time they were in St. Louis.
>
> This was all myself or nation knew of the treaty of 1804. It has been explained to me since. I find by that treaty all our country east of the Mississippi, and south of the Jefferson, was ceded to the United States for one thousand dollars a year! I leave it to the people of the United States to say whether our nation was properly represented in this treaty, or whether we received a fair compensation for the extent of country ceded those four individuals. I could say much about this treaty, but I will not at this time. It has been the origin of all our difficulties.

As early as 1817, the Indian agent Thomas Forsyth first broached the idea of moving west of the Mississippi to the Sauk. Yet, it was not until the 1820s that the U.S. government began forcefully enforcing the terms of the 1804 treaty. Drawn by the plentiful amounts of lead, many miners moved into southwestern Wisconsin and the Galena area in northwestern Illinois in the 1820s. The U. S.

government began to lease land in the Galena region, which violated the 1804 treaty. Though the Sauk protested this treaty violation, they succumbed to the power of the United States and allowed the miners to continue mining.

There would soon be reason for the U.S. government to finally fully enforce the terms of the Treaty of 1804 and force the Sauk across the Mississippi River. As early as 1823, squatters started to clear land for farming near Saukenuk. Pressure began building to open up more land in northern Illinois for settlement. Conflicts began to arise between the Sauk and the Americans as more settlers moved closer and closer to the Sauk, infringing on their lands. These settlers petitioned Governor Ninian Edwards of Illinois to remove the Indians.

Governor Edwards, governor from 1826-1830, wanted to remove all the Indians from Illinois land. Governor Edwards wrote to the secretary of war demanding that the Indians be removed to the west side of the Mississippi River. The Secretary of War, Peter B. Porter, promised that except for some Kickapoo, all the Indians would be removed west of the Mississippi by May 1829. The government surveyed the land adjacent to Saukenuk in 1828, and more squatters began to settle there. Saukenuk consisted of more than one hundred lodges, forty to sixty feet long, each occupied by several families. At that time, the total Sauk and Fox population was around 6000-7000, with about two-thirds being Sauk. In May 1828, Indian agent Thomas Forsyth told the Sauk they would have to relocate across the Mississippi by the following spring. Later that year, the Sauk and Fox left their village of Saukenuk, a few miles up from the mouth of the Rock River-today's Rock Island, Illinois-and moved west of the Mississippi to hunt for the winter. During the Sauk's absence, settlers began to move onto their occupied lands and into the temporarily vacated lodges. The settlers would soon have to contend with hostile Sauk.

In the spring of 1829, a portion of the Sauk and Fox returned under the leadership of Black Hawk. Black Hawk was one leader who always remained anti-American. Though not a civil chief, he earned much respect as a great warrior against the Osages, Cherokee, and other enemies. He directed war parties of more than five hundred warriors on long campaigns against faraway enemies when he was still a young man. During the War of 1812, he led two hundred Sauk and Fox to fight for the British. He participated in the Battle of the River Raisin and the Fort Meigs and Fort Stephenson sieges. In July 1813, he also led warriors in attacking reinforcements bound to besiege the British-held fort at Prairie du Chien (Battle of Campbell's Island). Then, with British assistance, he repelled the punitive expedition under Zachary Taylor (Battle of Credit Island). He even tried to continue warfare against the Americans after the British signed the Treaty of Ghent, ending the War of 1812.

Black Hawk and his followers found that settlers occupied many of their lodges. The Sauk and Fox moved into empty lodges and began planting their crops. Friction between the two peoples threatened to explode into serious violence. Forsyth again warned the Indians to leave the area. In July, the government announced it would put the land around Saukenuk up for public sale. Black Hawk's band finally departed, and Black Hawk declared that he would return the following spring. In October, 3000 acres, mainly in the Indian settlement area, were sold.

Keokuk assured Forsyth that the Sauk would not return in 1830. He had become a war chief of the Sauk during the War of 1812 while Black Hawk was away fighting with the British. Upon the rumored approach of an American force, Keokuk volunteered to lead the defense of a Saukenuk significantly weakened by the absence of so many warriors. He led a war party to confront the advancing Americans but did not encounter them. Ingratiating himself with William Clark, he obtained control of the Sauk annuities, thus gaining much power and control over the Sauk. As part of a delegation to Washington D.C. and other eastern cities, he realized that further resistance against the power of the United States was futile. His status and friendship with the United States would ensure that most of the Sauk would remain at peace.

Not so with Black Hawk, he lived up to his word and once again returned in 1830. A tense situation erupted as clashes between both peoples resulted when each group broke down fences and allowed their animals to wander into each other fields. Black Hawk's "British band," so named because of their British ties, stayed until the fall. When they left, Black Hawk said they would return the following spring. During the fall of 1830, Black Hawk sent his son and other emissaries to seek allies against the Americans among the Creeks, Cherokees, Osages, and other tribes, but they were unsuccessful in their mission.

When the Sauk reappeared in Illinois in 1831, Black Hawk only had one-sixth of the 6000 combined Sauk and Fox with him. At this time, the population of Illinois was over 150,000, and much of the northern part of the state was mostly clear of settlers. However, given the troubles of previous years, and since the Sauk insisted on returning to Saukenuk, the government brought military force to bear on them.

After Black Hawk refused appeals during negotiations with General Edmund Gaines to return across the Mississippi, Gaines requested help from Governor John Reynolds to force the removal of the Sauk. After receiving reinforcements of 1400 militia on the night of June 26, Gaines bombarded Saukenuk. Fortunately, Black Hawk's band had vacated the settlement the night before. Gaines again summoned Black Hawk and his followers and persuaded them to sign "articles of Agreement and Capitulation," whereby they promised never to return to Saukenuk. Black Hawk and his band then returned across the Mississippi. The settlers called this the "Corn Treaty" because Gaines had promised (not part of the treaty) that the settlers would provide the Indians with corn equivalent to that left in their fields so they would not starve the following Winter.

The settlers did not live up to the agreement, and the Indians grew restless. The Sauk resented the government's interference in their affairs, the continual trespassing of whites onto their lands, and the forceful eviction from their homes. For these reasons, some of Black Hawk's band encouraged him to lead them home again. His chief lieutenant, a warrior named Neapope, stated that the British would assist him. Wabokieshiek, the Winnebago prophet, assured him that the Potawatomi, Chippewas, and Ottawas would also aid him. Furthermore, he prophesied that if Black Hawk took up the hatchet once more against the whites, the Great Spirit would join him and a great army of worldlings, and in no time at all, he would banish the whites and be restored to his ancient village. So, in the end, determined to hold on to his home where he had been born, Black Hawk moved his band across the Mississippi on April 5, 1832.

Meanwhile, since the commander of the army's western department at St. Louis, Major General Edmund Gaines, was ill at Memphis, Tennessee, General Henry Atkinson was ordered to travel up the Mississippi with 220 men to arrest the Fox responsible for murdering Menominee Indians the previous year, and to prevent intertribal war from erupting between the Menominee and the Santee against the Fox. While on his journey up the Mississippi, Atkinson heard rumors that Black Hawk's band planned to reoccupy Saukenuk. Atkinson sent off a letter to Illinois Governor John Reynolds explaining the situation and mentioning the possibility of hostilities erupting.

Atkinson arrived at Fort Armstrong on April 11. Being on location, Atkinson would be responsible for commanding future war campaigns. He then spent three days talking to the Sauk Chief, Keokuk. Critics have said that if Atkinson had acted sooner in going after Black Hawk, bloodshed may have been averted. He had never experienced combat and would only command troops in the last battle during the upcoming war. Though Atkinson only had two hundred soldiers to pit against Black Hawk's five hundred warriors, he also could have drawn men from the garrisons at Fort Armstrong and Crawford. After Atkinson wrote Illinois Governor Reynolds of the situation, Reynolds immediately called out a volunteer army of 1200 militia.

Once crossing over the Mississippi, Black Hawk's band proceeded up the Rock River to Prophetstown in a week. During this movement, they did not take any hostile actions, no murders, no stealing, and no destruction of property. However, Atkinson learned in late April of dissension in the Sauk ranks when Sauk visitors told him that some members wanted to return to the West. Also, in early May six, canoes full of Sauk families deserted Black Hawk and came down the Rock River.

Despite dissension arising in his band, Black Hawk had rejected pleas to retreat across the Mississippi. Atkinson had sent two Sauk chiefs as couriers to urge Black Hawk to recross the Mississippi, telling him, "Some foolish people have told you that the British will assist you - do not believe it" "I advise you to come back and cross the Mississippi without delay. You will be sorry if you do not come back." Black Hawk replied that his band was peaceable and would not return and that his band was going further up the Rock River to settle with the Winnebago. In addition, Black Hawk rebuffed the Winnebago agent, Henry Gratiot, who relayed the same message to return across the Mississippi. Black Hawk hurt his chances for peace when he replied that he would fight if the army came after him. Also, Gratiot learned that Black Hawk had sent red wampum to the Winnebago, which was an invitation to join him in an alliance for war.

Perhaps war was inevitable. The highly respected historian of the times, R.G. Thwaites, has said that war may have been unavoidable.

"Conditions in Illinois were ripe for an Indian war. Many elements in the white population saw benefits from it. It would give occupation to the small but noisy class of pioneer loafer and cause money to circulate freely, to the numerous and respectable body of Indian-hater, and to persons who had at some time suffered from the red savages, and had come to regard them as little better than wild beasts, it offered a chance for reprisal. To the political aspirant, a brilliant foray presented opportunities for the achievement of personal popularity; indeed the Black Hawk War was long the chief stock in trade of many a subsequent statesman."

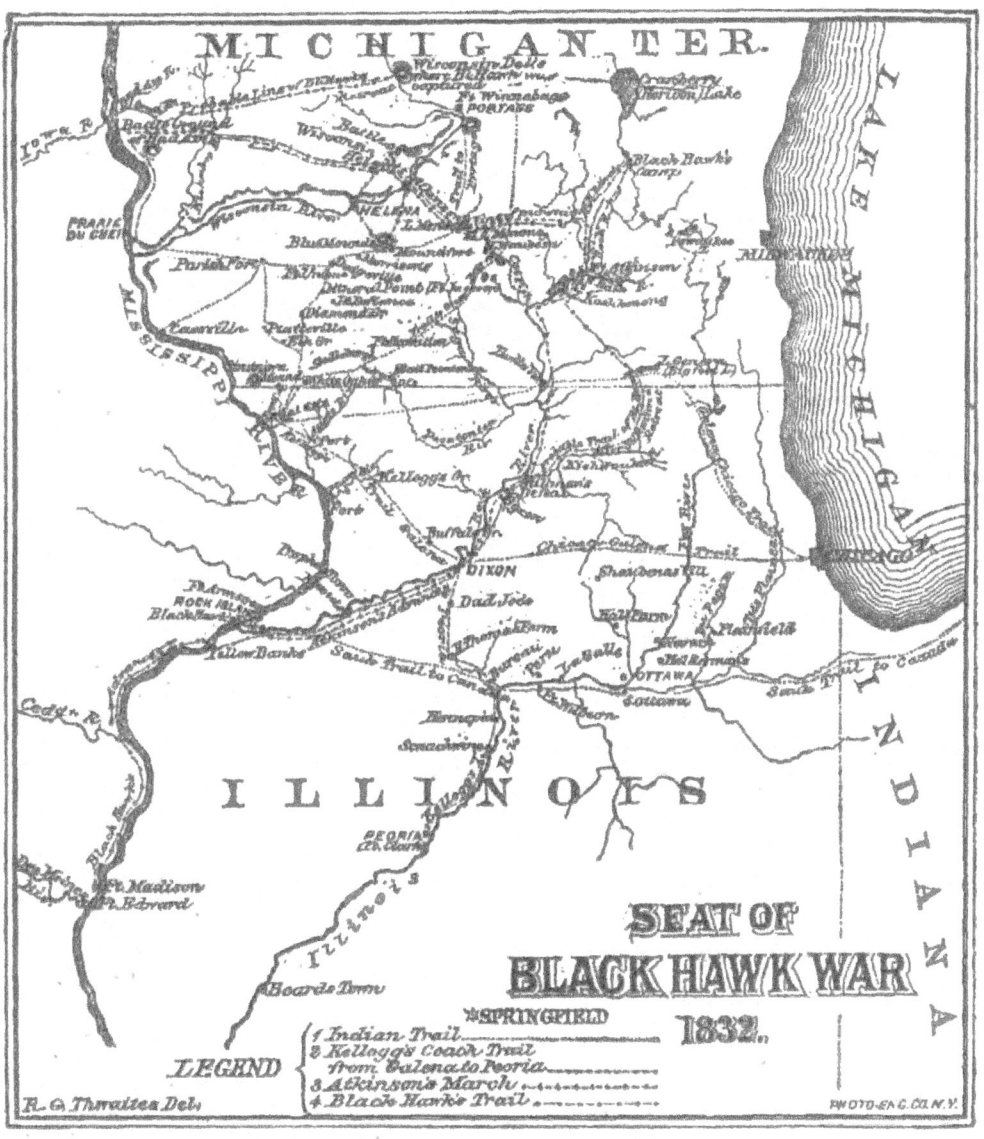

Chapter Fifteen

Stillman's Run

Wabokiesbiek, the Winnebago prophet, warned Black Hawk that the United States military was moving against his band. The Winnebago Prophet invited the Sauk to visit the Prophet's town to wait for further reinforcements. Black Hawk responded by moving his band of about one thousand women and children and about five hundred warriors (the number varies for the total size of the band from 1200-2000) another forty miles further up the Rock River. From the Prophet's village, the band moved further up the river to near present-day Rockford, Illinois, to meet with the Potawatomi and the Winnebago. In the meeting, Black Hawk finally realized that neither the British nor any other supposedly allied tribes would render him any assistance if it came to fighting. Since his band was now in a state of starvation and though Black Hawk feared that his band would be intercepted by the militia and possibly slaughtered, he decided to return to the Iowa side of the Mississippi. Because his people had not committed any hostile actions toward the whites, Black Hawk concluded that he could negotiate peace with the Americans.

Stillman's Run (American account, John A. Wakefield)

Meanwhile, Governor John Reynolds had called out the militia. Around two thousand men responded. With about 1500 of the militia joining his army of 1000 regulars, General Henry Atkinson had started in pursuit of Black

Hawk's band up the Rock River on May 10th. The first battle of the war, known as Stillman's Run, would be fought just four days later. The war could have been averted even at this late date, but it was not to be.

Under orders from Reynolds, Major Isaiah Stillman had raised a force of two hundred and seventy-five mounted volunteers and was currently in front of the army at Dixon's Ferry. Reynolds arrived there on May 12th. He learned from Stillman that Black Hawk's band was probably within thirty miles. Knowing that the volunteers had not been mustered into federal service yet, Reynolds, anxious to achieve glory, fraudulently had orders issued by Brigade Major Nathaniel Buckmaster to Stillman to move out to where it was believed Black Hawk's band was camped. This was done contrary to militia commander Samuel Whiteside's opposition. Though Atkinson had sent the volunteers in pursuit of Black Hawk's band and permitted them to move on the Indians before he arrived, Whiteside had refused Reynold's initial order, stating that if Atkinson thought 2000 troops were necessary to subdue the Indians, he wouldn't approve of two hundred for the task.

Once Black Hawk learned that not one of his supposed allies was coming to his aid and that the Americans were only about eight miles away from his camp, he sent three braves with a white flag toward Stillman's command to seek permission for his band to descend the Rock River and return to Iowa.

John A Wakefield, a militiaman, volunteer scout, and a surgeon's mate who served throughout the Black Hawk War, gives the following account of what happened next. It illustrates the fears and exaggerations expressed about an enemy by panicky men.

> On our arrival here (Dixon's Ferry) we found Major Stillman with a battalion of two hundred and seventy-five men awaiting our arrival:

they had been there two days with a sufficient supply of ammunition and provisions; our provisions at this time being nearly exhausted.

Major Stillman considered that he had a kind of independent corps, and did not wish to be attached to General Whiteside's Brigade. He, the Major, on the next morning made a request of the Governor, that he might be permitted to take his corps, go out as a scouting party, and see whether any discoveries could be made as to the situation of the enemy.

Accordingly, on the 12th day of May, Major Stillman and Major David Bailey received orders from the Commander in Chief, to march with their respective battalions to the neighborhood of Old Man's Creek, to ascertain, if possible, the movements of the enemy. On the morning of the 13th, Major Stillman's battalion took up their line of march. Major Bailey followed in a short time after; and after having marched eight or ten miles, both battalions encamped. The day had been rainy, and other circumstances beyond the control of officers or men, had a tendency to retard their movements.

The battalions had no connection with each other whatever, previous to their meeting on their march to Dixon's, on Rock river. There they received orders to march, before they were organized into a regiment--each battalion being independent of the other--commanded by its own officers--and three of those claiming the command of both--and perhaps with equal justice.

In the result, however, the command for that expedition was conferred on Major Stillman, the choice of officers to be referred to the men on their return.

On the morning of the 14th, under the temporary organization of the corps, the march was continued in the line, secured by the strong advance and flank guards. On this day's march several fresh trails were discovered during the forenoon; and at 12 o'clock the commanding officer, was informed, that several Indian dogs had been seen by one of the flank guards, and shortly afterwards two Indians were seen.

With some difficulty occasioned by the almost impassable mires of the creeks which the corps had to cross, the march was continued until nearly sunset, when Col. Strode of the advanced guard, who had volunteered his services on this occasion, returned to the battalion with the information of a suitable place for encampment, and conducted the corps to the point.

A large fresh trail was discovered, which directed its course to a point of timber, a sort distance to the left of the encampment. Shortly after the battalion halted, and while busily engaged in preparing supper, several horsemen were discovered on a hill about half mile in front. They were at first sight taken for a part of the enemy's advance guard. Some of the men mounted their horses, and rode toward them. They were discovered to be Indians, and two of them came to the camp, professing to be Pottawattomies and friends, but on the approach of our advance the Indians gave a whoop, unfurled a red flag and fell back at full speed.--Our horsemen followed, and after a chase of four miles and a half, overtook them in a low marshy piece of ground, where a sharp firing took place. Three Indians were left dead, and several were dismounted; one of our men was wounded in a personal combat, and two were dismounted and lost their horses.

The Indians were driven into their encampment, where they rallied to the number of six or eight hundred, and cautiously awaited the approach of our main body. Our advance fell back, and joined the battalion on the margin of the low ground, where the firing first commenced.

An Indian approached and proposed a "talk" to an officer who was in advance. Major Stillman with the field and staff officers together with Capt. Eads as an interpreter, went forward while the troops were advancing by heads of companies through the marsh. Capt. Eads, who had been in front, suddenly wheeled and exclaimed that the line of Indians extended for more than a mile.

Major Stillman now discovered that the proposed "talk" was an expedient to obtain time, the more completely to execute their plan; for the enemy were now seen flanking him right and left in great numbers. He immediately gave orders to countermarch and form on the high ground. But instead of countermarching, the men wheeled about in their places, which threw the officers all in the rear, and fell back. The foremost of them on reaching the hard ground first, were able to proceed with much greater rapidity than those who were yet in the swamp, and by the time the officers reached the solid ground the front was out of hearing. The order to halt and form was only heard by a part of each company, who immediately formed. But the enemy knew all the passes, and had already opened a heavy fire on both flanks, which was returned with spirit by those who had formed.

It was now found necessary to retire to prevent the enemy from entirely surrounding our men, which had now become practicable. The retreat was then kept up with occasional halting and firing, until our men reached the camp. There, an attempt was made to maintain our ground. Capt. Barnes had nearly succeeded in forming his company, when orders were given to cross the creek in rear of the camp. This order was effected by sixty or seventy men, but not before the enemy had got possession of the camp. The enemy then set up a tremendous yell, which was returned by a volley of musketry from those who had formed in the rear of the camp,--this silenced the war-whoop in that quarter, but in a moment more two large parties of the enemy, who had crossed the creek above and below, attacked both flanks and the rear. The line was broken, and each man took his own course. One party broke off to the right where fell some of those who had formed at the creek. Another party took off to the left, where others fell, the flanking parties of the enemy pursuing them. Those of the men who took the middle course, escaped with the loss of two killed, and one wounded

The enemy kept up the pursuit for twelve or fourteen miles. The men arrived at Dixon's ferry in detached squads, from one o'clock A. M. until the roll call at sunrise, when it was found that fifty-two were missing: these continued to arrive for the two succeeding days, until the number missing was reduced to eleven, which were afterward found most shockingly mangled.

Capt. Adams evinced the most undaunted bravery; he vehemently urged the men to maintain the ground. But the line was broken and he himself was slain.

Several personal encounters took place. In one of them Joseph Farris and his brother David, were attacked and surrounded. David was mounted, and Joseph whose horse failed or was killed, urged him to save himself; but this he refused, until he saw him fall, fighting, and himself struck from his horse by a blow from the breech of a gun. He returned the blow which stiffened the savage on the ground, and then broke for a point of timber; he was nearly overtaken, when he called for assistance from the timber, which led the pursuers to fear that a force was then awaiting their approach. It was this presence of mind which saved his life; for the enemy immediately wheeled and retreated...

Major Stillman was unfortunate in this action; he lost some of his most choice men. Captain Adams, who commanded a company from Tazewell county; Major Isaac Perkins; John Walters; Cyrus Childs; Joseph Farris; Bird Ellis and James Doty, were among the slain in this battle. There were four others, but I have not got in possession of their names. They were all respectable men.

When this squadron of men got into camp, or part of them, for they came in by twos, threes and fours, and so on, all night, each company thought the rest were all killed, and reported it as being the case.

We were all immediately to our arms, not knowing but that Black Hawk and all his band were in close pursuit.

Things were represented in their worst colors. Some of the men seemed to think that there were at least two thousand Indians. Others thought there were not more than one thousand, and none would fall below five hundred; but scarcely any two of them could agree upon any one statement.

It was a complete rout, and of course each one had to shift for himself; and it was natural for them to have different views when they were in such frightful condition. Next morning, at roll call, there were fifty-two men missing. It was then thought there was no doubt but they had all been slain in the action; but to the great joy of the friends of the missing, they all got in, in the course of three days, to some settlement or other, except the eleven already mentioned. It appears that they were so much alarmed, that they took different directions, and some went a contrary direction from the army. A number of them, it is said, came very near starving with hunger before they got to any settlement.

Many volunteers deserted after Stillman's defeat. Only about three hundred stayed on for another twenty days, and Abraham Lincoln was among those who stayed.

Zachary Taylor said to Atkinson of Stillman's defeat: "The more I see of the militia the less confidence I have of their effecting anything of importance; and therefore tremble not only for the safety of the frontiers, but for the reputation of those who command them, who have any reputation to lose."

Stillman's Run (Black Hawk's Account)

According to Black Hawk, he had moved up the Rock River seeking the aid of the Winnebagos. They declined to ally with him against the Americans. He then moved further up the river to meet with the Potawatomi. They also refused to aid him, not even refusing to provide food for the hungry band. They also informed Black Hawk that the British would not assist him either. With no hope of aid from any allies and shortage of supplies, Black Hawk realized further resistance was futile. Black Hawk decided he had no choice but to make peace with the Americans.

The next day, Black Hawk's scouts informed him that Stillman's men were only eight miles away. He then sent three of his braves out as ambassadors to try to negotiate with the Americans. Another five followed them to watch. The first three entered Stillman's camp in the early evening. When the militia saw the other five braves observing from a distance, they concluded that an attack was imminent. Immediately, they raced toward the five warriors and shot two of them. The rest escaped and informed Black Hawk while he was in the midst of a ceremonial feast with his Potawatomi guests. Meanwhile, the militia killed one of the three ambassadors, and the other two escaped.

Black Hawk reacted angrily that his men had been murdered under a flag of truce. He only had about forty warriors who were present with him, but he yelled out to them, "Some of our people have been killed! We must revenge their death!" His Potawatomi guests immediately departed. In his own words, Black Hawk describes what happened next.

> In a little while we discovered the whole army coming towards us in full gallop! We were confident that our first party had been killed! I immediately placed my men in front of some bushes, that we might have the first fire, when they approached close enough. They made a halt some distance from us. I gave another yell, and ordered my brave warriors to charge upon them- -expecting that we would all be killed! They did charge! Every man rushed and fired, and the enemy retreated! in the utmost confusion and consternation, before my little, but brave band of warriors!

Black Hawk lost three men during the fighting, and he sought revenge for their deaths. The war had now begun. Black Hawk's band of about five hundred warriors were arrayed against thousands of soldiers and militia in Illinois and the surrounding states. Black Hawk sent the women, the children, and the older men to the Lake Koshkonong region in south and central Wisconsin and divided his warriors into small groups of raiders. He led the largest group of about two hundred warriors. Due to his victory over Stillman's militia, small parties of Winnebago and about one hundred Potawatomi joined him.

Because of the Stillman debacle, many settlers fled in fear of more Indian attacks and fled to safer, more populated areas (such as Chicago). About four hundred and fifty men, women, and children sought refuge in Chicago after receiving warnings from runners sent out by Indian agent Thomas Owen. Other settlers chose to fort up, quickly constructing forts at Galena, Apple River, Kellogg's Grove, Buffalo Grove, Dixon's, South Ottawa, Hennepin, and several other locations in Illinois and Wisconsin. They would not have to wait long before the Indians struck.

On Indian Creek, William Davis built a sawmill, and a small settlement was established. By creating a dam across the creek for the sawmill, Davis had aggravated the nearby Potawatomi village because the dam hindered the migration of the fish upstream. The Potawatomi protested to Davis due to the depletion of their food supply caused by his action, but he ignored their protests. When one Potawatomi tried to destroy the dam, Davis caught and thrashed him.

Shabonna, a Potawatomi chief friendly to the Americans, warned the settlers at Indian Creek on May 21 that they were in danger of possible attack. About half of the settlers fled to a fort at Ottawa, about twelve miles to the south. On that same day, in a surprise attack on the settlement, about fifty Potawatomi killed fifteen men, women, and children. They took two prisoners, teenagers Sylvia and Rachel Hall, who were later released.

Some other Indians took advantage to settle scores against the Americans. One small party of Kickapoo who had left Black Hawk's band after Stillman's Run burned cabins and committed other outrages against settlers. Also, a small Winnebago party of thirteen attacked seven whites at Kellogg's Grove, killing four of them. There were several other attacks on isolated settlers in Northeastern Illinois until late June, when Black Hawk's band retreated into Wisconsin. One even occurred as far east as present-day Naperville, Illinois, when a small party of warriors killed an Illinois volunteer near Fort Payne. This killing was probably committed by Potawatomi sympathetic to Black Hawk.

However, Potawatomi leadership was committed to remaining at peace with the Americans. They had seen the power of the United States and did not want to do anything that would affect their annuities. To prevent additional young warriors from joining Black Hawk or committing any further hostilities against Americans, they gathered them in a camp along the Des Plaines River in Riverside, Illinois.

News of the Black Hawk War quickly traveled east. In June, the National Intelligencer proclaimed that "the whole frontier was in a complete state of alarm and confusion." Being an election year, President Andrew Jackson wanted Black Hawk defeated quickly. He did not want to endure the criticism of his administration and feared that Black Hawk's example could induce the Potawatomi, Winnebago, Santee Sioux, and other tribes to hostile actions. Since General Atkinson's efforts had thus far appeared to be ineffective in defeating Black Hawk, he dispatched General Winfield Scott, a hero from the War of 1812, to Illinois to take over command from Atkinson.

While shipping on his way up the Hudson River in New York with eight hundred soldiers, cholera broke out on board. When he arrived in Chicago on July 10, only one hundred fifty of his men were fit for duty. Scott ordered the evacuation of Fort Dearborn and set up a hospital there for the men. The arrival of the diseased men caused a panic in Chicago, and many of the residents fled the city. Scott's decision to stay in Chicago to care for his men allowed Atkinson to remain in command and conduct the rest of the campaign against Black Hawk.

Chapter Sixteen

Kellogg's Grove

After Stillman's Run, Atkinson sent out scouting parties searching for Black Hawk's band. He recruited many of these scouts from the Potawatomi, Winnebago, Santee Sioux, and Menominee tribes, who served as auxiliaries. The Menominee were particularly eager to participate so they could take revenge on the Fox Indians who had massacred their brethren the prior year and who were accompanying Black Hawk's band. William S. Hamilton, the son of Alexander Hamilton, commanded these scouts, eventually two hundred and twenty-five in all. Unfortunately, much of their talent was wasted searching for Black Hawk in the wrong area. He had heard of burning abandoned cabins along the Fox and Du page Rivers and sent them in that direction. Due to lack of action, many of the scouts quit after a short time.

While the search was on for Black Hawk, the strategic advantages of Kellogg's Grove quickly impressed the mind of General Atkinson. In 1832, the buildings of Kellogg's Grove were comprised of log cabins, a barn (large for those days), and outbuildings to the number of seven, strung along one hundred and twenty feet, each approximating seven feet in height, sixteen in length, and all covered with basswood bark. Today, a monument is erected near present-day Kent, Illinois, in Stephenson County, about thirty-five miles southeast of Galena, thirty-seven miles north of Dixon, and seven or eight miles from Lena.

As marauding Indians from Black Hawk's band began their incursions into the surrounding territory,

Atkinson's first thought for distributing his new twenty-day troops was to send a company of strong men and establish a base for operations between Dixon's Ferry and Galena—the company of Capt. Adam W. Snyder, of sixty-nine men, was selected for that hazardous duty. Almost concurrently, Captain Iles' company marched from the mouth of the Fox River for Dixon's Ferry. In Captain Snyder's company, as privates, were the late Joseph Gillespie, Pierre Menard, Richard Roman, James Semple, Gen. Samuel Whiteside, and Hugh Thomas, just elected Major, whose headquarters were properly opposite the mouth of Fox River with the other regimental officers. Still preferring the dangers and privations of the field, he resumed his private position under Captain Snyder and marched in the ranks.

At Dixon's Ferry, Captain Iles' company was detached for a separate duty. Still, Brevet-Major Bennet Riley, with two companies of regulars, accompanied the Snyder expedition to Kellogg's Grove. Without any event on the road thither, other than the death of Private Loren Cleveland on June 12th, it quickly reached its destination.

Remaining there briefly, Captain Snyder left Riley and the regulars behind and pushed on to Galena to familiarize himself with the country. He arrived at Galena on June 13th at about noon. The following day, he returned to Kellogg's Grove. The following is the account of Frank E. Stevens from his book *The Black Hawk War*.

On the night of June 15th the troops were snugly ensconced in the various buildings, after sentinels had been picketed about eighty yards out at different points of the compass around the camp. The night was cloudy and dark, though intermittently illuminated with flashes of lightning, rendering possible a sight of the surroundings during those periods. Near midnight the presence of the enemy was deleted by a sentinel, who in the instantaneous period allowed him, attempted to run the Indian he discovered through with his bayonet, so close had he crawled; but the flash of light was so brief that the sentinel missed his mark and only rubbed the Indian's arm. Dropping his gun, the sentinel clinched with his adversary and by reason of superior strength was rapidly mastering him and would soon have had him a prisoner, but for another flash which discovered two other Indians within twenty feet, making for the rescue as rapidly as the impenetrable darkness would permit. Quickly releasing his antagonist, the sentinel ran to camp, shouting: "Indians, Indians," while the Indians pursued him as far as they dared. With a shot into the darkness they turned and fled, leaving the men in camp to lie upon their arms after that until morning.

From the fact that one horse was stolen during the night, color was given to the theory that plunder was the sole aim of the enemy's presence, but events of the following day exploded it.

Early in the morning Captain Snyder took a detachment of his men and pursued the enemy's trail in a southwesterly direction, hoping to overtake and punish him before escape was possible. For twenty miles it was followed in vain, but Captain Snyder would not permit it to be abandoned, and wise indeed was his decision, for after a few rods more of travel the detachment came upon four of the Indians preparing a meal in a deep ravine just ahead. Flight by them in a circuitous, back-track manner was instantly taken, which nearly baffled the troops, but after another weary but exciting chase the Indians were again discovered half a mile ahead climbing a high hill within three miles of camp at Kellogg's Grove. The troops were delayed in their pursuit by a deep and muddy creek, but on finally crossing it discovered the Indians firmly intrenched in a deep gulch, where , in a sharp hand to hand encounter, all four were killed, with loss to the whites of one man, private William B. Mecomson (or Mekemson), who received two balls in the abdomen, inflicting a mortal wound. While the engagement lasted it was a fierce and wicked a frontier fight as has ever been recorded, and in the many shots exchanged by the Indians the marvel is that the loss to the whites was no greater; but poor Mecomson received the only effective ones.

A litter was constructed of poles and blankets, upon which the wounded man was placed and, carried by his comrades, he was conveyed toward camp. In ministering to his needs his bearers were compelled to deliver their guns and horses to the keeping of others, the exchange and relief causing some delay and a little temporary confusion; men were necessarily scattered along with no regard for order; the troops were flushed with the first victory of the campaign, and while danger was to be at all times apprehended, having disposed of one enemy, the presence of other Indians was not a very strong probability. Thus the men marched along for three-quarters of a mile, when the dying man asked for a brief rest and a cup of water. As no fresh water was carried, two squads were detailed by Captain Snyder to search for some. General Whiteside, First Sergeant Nathan Johnston and Third Sergeant James Taylor went to one side, while Dr. Richard Roman, Benjamin Scott, Second Corporal Benjamin McDaniel, Dr. Francis Jarrott and Dr. I.M. McTy Cornelius searched the other side for water with which to quench the wounded man's thirst. While the last named squad was moving slowly down a ridge to a point having a bushy ravine on each side it was fired on by a large party of Indians, instantly killing Benjamin Scott and Benjamin McDaniel and slightly wounding Dr. Cornelius. The three survivors retreated while the Indians, estimated from fifty to ninety in number, hideously yelling, rushed upon poor Mecomson and chopped off his head with a tomahawk; then wheeling, they directed their fire upon the main body of the whites, who were somewhat scattered, as stated. Closing in as well as possible, the detachment fell back in good order, formed again and returned a brisk fire, which checked the enemy's advance. Quickly following up the advantage gained, Captain Snyder moved rapidly forward, bringing his men at close range with the enemy and making the engagement general. Trees were many times used for protection. During the thickest of the fight the apparent leader of the Indians, mounted on a white horse, rode backward and forward, urging his men on with shouts and gestures; but the intrepid volunteers were pouring lead into the ranks of the Indians with such deadly effect that they were gradually forced back. After a little the white horse was seen leaving the field without a rider; at the same time the Indians temporarily wavered and the whites pushed their lines closer. The Indians, having evidently lost their leader, sullenly retired out of range and Captain Snyder held his advanced position.

Major Thomas had in the meantime volunteered to go alone to Kellogg's Grove, less than three miles distant, for reinforcements from Major Riley, and though the trip was perilous in the extreme he made it safely, returning in an incredibly short time with the reinforcements. When they arrived Captain Snyder had driven the Indians to the timber and was anxious to press his advantage, but the lateness of the hour prevented. He then insisted on camping on the spot for the night, that he might pursue his advantage early in the morning, but Major Riley persuaded him to return to camp at Kellogg's which he reluctantly did after gathering up the dead for burial the following day.

Early the following morning Captain Snyder, with his full company, returned to the scene of the previous day's engagements in search of the enemy, but he was nowhere to be found, and burying the dead, the company at once returned to camp, where it remained a few days longer, by which time the new levies having been rapidly massed at Dixon's Ferry for the final struggle, Captain Snyder marched to that point, and his company was mustered out by Colonel Taylor on June 21.

Waddam's Grove

Indians stole horses just outside Apple River Fort on June 8 and 17. After the second incident, the attempt to recover them would lead to another minor battle fought at Waddam's Grove (also known as the Battle of Yellow Creek. Stevens describes the action as follows:

> Horsestealing became a recognized feature of Black Hawk's campaign very soon after Stillman's defeat, which he pushed with unusual vigor. He would snatch a band of horses, and if the luckless owner attempted a pursuit for their recovery he was invariably ambushed. On the night of June 8th the Indians stole fourteen horses just outside the stockade of Apple River fort (now Elizabeth, Illinois), and on the afternoon and night of the 17th ten more were stolen. The number was so large and the loss so great that unusual measures

were adopted to attempt their recovery. As nothing but a military escort was considered equal to the search, Captain J.W. Stephenson, with twelve men from Galena and nine from Apple River Fort, started on the trail early on the morning of the 18th, and overtook the thieves about twelve miles east of Kellogg's Grove, on the Yellow River, southeast of Waddam's Grove, in Stephenson County. A hot pursuit followed for several miles. The Indians, seven in number, finally reaching a dense thicket, plunged into it for protection. The thicket, a short distance northeast of Waddam's Grove was so dense that it was impossible to discover their location from the open country surrounding it, and thus secreted the Indians remained awaiting the attack of the whites. Stephenson was impatient to dislodge them by assault. Dismounting his men, he at first attempted to sweep the thicket and draw the enemy's fire, but the witty Indians refused to shoot or otherwise indicate their position. Discarding strategy as an evidence of cowardice, Captain Stephenson detailed a guard for the horses, and with his remaining men made an impetuous charge upon the hidden reds, drawing their fire and returning it, but with the loss of one to the whites as they were retiring to the prairie to reload. Rather than accept the loss and carefully continue the assault by safer and surer methods, Captain Stephenson twice more charged the fatal thicket, losing one man with each effort, while the Indians lost but one man, who was stabbed in the neck by Thomas Sublet. Both sides had exhausted their loads in the charge and the fight became general and at close range; so close, indeed, that one could scarcely distinguish friend from foe, and rather than continue against odds entirely conjectural, the whites withdrew again to the prairie to consult-precaution they should have exercised in the first instance.

Captain Stephenson himself was wounded so seriously that he was no longer able to continue in command. Of the whites, Stephen P. Howard, Charles Eames and Michael Lovell had been killed, while the Indians had lost but the one man, and he had not been killed by guns. Further assaults were considered useless, and, if continued, would have been willful; therefore, leaving the dead where they fell, the men returned to Galena for assistance to return and bury the three dead soldiers and the Indian, reaching that point on the 19th.

Chapter Seventeen

Apple River Fort and Second Battle of Kellogg's Grove

After Stillman's defeat, panic occurred across much of northern Illinois and southern Wisconsin. Settlers fortified their homes, erected blockhouses, and gathered for safety or, in fear for their lives, fled. For example, in Plainfield, Illinois, approximately sixty miles from Stillman's defeat, residents forted up at the home of Rev. Stephen R. Beggs. They later fled to Chicago after hearing of the Indian Creek Massacre in LaSalle County, where fifteen men, women, and children of the Hall, Davis, and Pennigre families were murdered. Two of the Hall girls, Rachel and Sylvia, were hauled into captivity and later ransomed.

One such place where residents fortified was the Apple River Settlement at present-day Elizabeth, Illinois. In an unusual endeavor, citizen residents gathered to erect a stockade and build a fort around existing cabins without any military assistance. According to one author, they built the fort in a day. The fort was tiny. The residents enclosed a 48' by 68' 6" area (3,000 square feet) with walls 12 feet high around the cabins. The logs used for the stockade have been estimated at approximately 8" to 10" in diameter, in which case about 250 would have been required to construct the walls. The logs were irregular and varied in size. The space in between them allowed the men to fire through them. Several sentinel stands were built along the wall. Two log houses were on the southwest and northeast corners. One was converted into a two-story blockhouse as well. There were probably several crude small shanties or huts within the wall and tents for shelter. In addition, several buildings were near the fort. In preparation for hostilities, the settlers collected foodstuffs into the fort, gathered other necessary supplies, molded extra bullets, and cast a crude cannon made from lead. By May 23, they had finished preparing for an Indian attack. During the day, families went to their homesteads; at night, they returned to the safety of the fort. Twenty-two men, mostly miners, and twenty-three women and children, resided in the fort.

In the ensuing days, Indians stole horses from a corral outside the fort; on June 8, they stole fourteen horses and again, on June 17, took off with ten more. The settler's fear of attack would become a reality on the evening of June 24, 1832. Unbeknown to them, Black Hawk and between 150 to 200 warriors arrived in the afternoon. They would soon be making the only attack on a fort led by Black Hawk during the four-month war.

The following account of the battle is that of Frank E. Stevens:

> On Sunday morning, the 24th day of June, Colonel Strode sent an express of three men, Fredrick Dixon, Edmund Welch and one Kirkpatrick, with dispatches for General Atkinson, then at Dixon's Ferry. By reason of the drenching rain falling at the time of their departure, the men discharged their muskets upon starting out.
>
> Arrived at Apple River fort, twelve or fourteen miles southeast from Galena, at about noon, the express found there Capt. Clack Stone, the commandant, with only fifteen or twenty of his command with him, the others being absent on detached service. The women of the post were all out along the river, gathering berries, or else just starting for that purpose, clearly indicating that war

was furthest from their thoughts. Pausing but a moment to pass the news from Galena and allow Mr. Welch to reload his musket, the express again started forward and had covered about too yards to the east, when Mr. Welch, who had gained about fifty yards on his companions, was suddenly fired on by a large party of Indians concealed in the high grass near a point necessary to pass on his journey. Rising instantly, they were on the point of seizing and scalping him, as he fell from his horse, shot through the thigh, when he quickly rose and fired at his assailants, some fifteen steps away. His shot was ineffectual, his horse fled, and he would surely have perished had not his companions rushed to his rescue and saved him. They had no loads to fire, but used their guns in a series of feints as though to shoot. The Indians dodged and cowered until the men were able to gain the fort, and there secure protection for two of the number. Mr. Dixon, in his frantic efforts to secure the safety of the wounded man, paid no attention to his own welfare, and though he saw Kirkpatrick slip within, did not consider himself until the heavy timbered door slammed in his face, leaving him to face the Indians, who by this time were upon him in overwhelming numbers. Dixon was a redoubtable man and full of the resources needed in a new country, and without an instant's loss he mounted, wheeled, and made for the timber, whose hidden paths he thoroughly knew. The Indians must have been more intent upon the scalps of the little garrison and plunder of the many substantial homes of the neighborhood than Dixon, for they quickly abandoned him altogether, but he, on reaching the house of Mr. John McDonald, where he expected certain relief and safety, found it filled with Indians and himself surrounded. Abandoning his horse, he fled to the rear, followed the margin of Apple River, under cover of its high bank, and, after traveling all night, reached Galena in the morning, painfully bruised and exhausted, but not so tired as to prevent his wish and determination to return to the rescue of his friends.

The shots by the Indians warned all of approaching danger and gave them time to leave the berries and the river and gain the fort, but no sooner were they all safely "forted" than the Indians, who had been massing from all points of the compass to the number of at least 200, surrounded it and hurled against the fort a terrific fire.

Providentially, a wagonload of meat and lead from Galena had been unloaded that very forenoon, which put the garrison in a tolerable state to sustain a siege.

For two hours a heavy fire was maintained by both sides. Under its first fire, the garrison showed fear of the result against such tremendous odds, but instantly Mrs. Elizabeth Armstrong, in a commanding address, inspired man and woman alike with such resolution that nothing could have driven them from their posts. She divided the women into two squads, one to mold bullets, the other to reload the muskets as they were discharged Unfortunately, no time had been allowed to bring in a supply of water with which to quench thirst during the weary hours of that engagement The day was hot. Confinement in close quarters of the fort, amidst the fumes of gunpowder and heat of the firing, brought on a state of suffering bordering upon exhaustion, but the almost fainting women, by their heroic disregard for danger and suffering, and by their words of cheer, propped the failing energies of the fighting men. Every advance by the enemy was met with a galling fire from within and the assailants were repulsed, only to resume the assault more fiercely than before and again retire with heavy loss.

Finding it useless to attempt a capitulation by assault, the Indians retired to the surrounding log houses, where, knocking the chinks from between the logs, they opened a deadly fire, which could not be returned with loss to themselves; but this failed to dislodge the whites, and, enraged at their failure, the Indians sought partial revenge by plundering the houses. They destroyed the furniture and crockery, emptied flour barrels and feather beds, stole the bed clothing and wardrobe and then killed the cattle and hogs, finishing their day of destruction stealing all the horses in sight.

As night approached, Kirkpatrick, who was but a boy, resolved upon going to Galena to seek the aid which he was fearful his companion would never live to obtain. Remonstrances were of no avail, and he set out on his perilous journey in the blackness of the night. With a courage and skill known only on the frontier, he pushed bravely through, reaching Galena in time to meet Colonel Strode as he was starting out with Dixon and his relief party for the fort.

Strode moved rapidly down and left such reinforcements as were needed, but the Indians troubled Apple River fort no more. The heroic little garrison had driven them away for all time.

This band, under Black Hawk's leadership, was supposed, with good reason, to be the same that attacked Major Dement at Kellogg's Grove on the 25th. George W. Herclerode, who exposed his head too much in taking aim, and was shot through the neck and instantly killed, and James Nutting, wounded, were the only casualties to the whites.

Black Hawk, in his autobiography, stated that he broke off the attack because:

> Finding that these people could not all be killed, without setting fire to their homes and fort, I thought it more prudent to be content with what flour, provisions, cattle and horses we could find, then to set fire to their buildings, as the light would be seen at a distance, and the army might suppose that we were in the neighborhood, and come upon us with a force to strong. Accordingly, we opened a house and filled our bags with flour and provisions-took several horses and drove off some of their cattle.

Second Battle of Kellogg's Grove

Following the attack on Apple River Fort, Black Hawk's band of an estimated two hundred warriors moved away from the fort. The next day, they went to the east, where they encountered Major John Dement's militia force and fought the Second Battle of Kellogg's Grove. Just the day before the battle, Colonel Zachary Taylor, who believed the militia were good for nothing, had criticized the Illinois militia virtually accusing them of cowardice. He then concluded his speech with the words: "You are citizen soldiers and some of you may fill high offices, or even be President some day, but never unless you do your duty Forward! March!" These were prophetic words! Taylor became President, and Jefferson Davis, his aide, was present. Abraham Lincoln, the second President to be elected from that little army, arrived soon after with Henry's Brigade.

Stevens' account of this small battle where Dement's militia, consisting of men who had held nearly every office in the State, from the Governor on down, fought similarly to any other militia is as follows:

At daylight of the 25th Major Dement called for twenty-five volunteers to reconnoiter, and these instantly responded and moved out. Just as Dement and Lieutenant Governor Zadock Casey were mounting their horses an express came in from the advance party, informing them that three or four Indians were seen on the prairie. This information operated like an electric shock on the men, and the orders, so careful elaborated were cast to the winds as one and all, regardless of order, security, experience or common sense, dashed after the reported Indians helter-skelter. Though Dement tried times without number, at the risk of his life, to bring the troops off in good order, his efforts were unavailing. Refusing to learn from the experience of Stillman, the foremost men dashed headlong on to some timber where Dement had surmised the enemy was concealed. He shouted to his men to beware, but once more old Black Hawk's videttes decoyed the whites to destruction. About four hundred yards from Kellogg's, Major Dement halted and formed a line to await the charge he was positive would follow, and he had not long to wait. Stillman's fight was to be duplicated in large measure, and by Black Hawk, too, for he was personally leading his men. Just as the whites neared the edge of the timber, the enemy opened a galling fire, which killed two men and wounded a third; then, with hideous yells, a large force poured from the grove to the right and left, to flank the little band about Major Dement. The Indians, all well mounted, were stripped to the skin and painted. As they reached the bodies of the dead soldiers they clubbed, scalped and otherwise mutilated them in the usual way.

Major Dement stood his ground, firing volley after volley with deadly effect into the advancing ranks of the enemy, but the Indians continued to put from the timber until the whites realized that delay in their perilous position meant willful death. Then they wheeled about, and a most exciting race for life began, with the Indians on both flanks fighting at every step and gaining at every foot of the tase. Then happened a melancholy event. Three men, whose horses had strayed away during the night, had early in the morning started in search of them, and, returning, were caught in one of the flanks of the enemy, who swept over and killed them in an instant, after which every man was scalped, but, to their everlasting honor, no three men ever sold their lives at heavier cost to the enemy than they, for five dead Indians were found close to their bodies.

During this tragic respite, Major Dement rallied a few men about him and made another stand to give the shrieking savages battle, but it was momentary only; the men caught but a sight of the returning enemy and abandoned their intrepid little commander to his fate. At the last and supreme moment he dashed to cover and only reached it by a neck.

In this engagement Governor Casey's horse was badly wounded and his escape was made only after a terrific fight with the enemy. Reaching Kellogg's, the men sprang from their horses and occupied the log house and barn. On the least exposed side of the house was a workbench, over which Major Dement threw his bridle, and shot through an open window; into this same partially sheltered place the horses instinctively huddled.

As the Indians swarmed into the grove and covered themselves behind trees, portholes were made in the chinks of the log buildings and the best shots were detailed to pick off the Indians who might expose themselves, but very few of them were so rash. For many hours the garrison was stormed, it being apparently the determination of Black Hawk to exterminate the battalion to the last man, as he assailed it again and again, the Indians becoming finally careless of their security as the assault progressed. Making no impression on the besieged, the enemy finally began the merciless butchery of the horses, killing above twenty-five in their savage rage.

The reinforcements sent for were, fortunately, near at hand, for Posey's Brigade had that very morning been ordered to march, and was then actually in motion for Kellogg's Grove, on its way to Fort Hamilton to join General Dodge. The Indians finally retired, leaving nine dead on the field, and escaped with others, before the arrival of Posey, who had met Lieut. Trammel Ewing, who, though shot through the thigh, had offered to start for Dixon's for reinforcements and had met Posey north of Buffalo Grove. When he delivered his dispatches to General Posey that officer hastened to the scene with incredible swiftness, while Lieutenant Ewing journeyed on to Dixon to carry the news.

Black Hawk in his own autobiography, Second Ed. p. 104, in noticing this battle and Major Dement, used the following language: "The chief, who seemed to be a small man, addressed his warriors in a loud voice, but they soon retreated, leaving him and a few braves on the battlefield.:

"A great number of my warriors pursued the retreating party and killed a number of their horses as they ran."

"The chief and a few of his braves were unwilling to leave the field. I ordered my braves to rush upon them, and had the mortification go seeing two of my chiefs killed before the enemy retreated."

"The young chief deserves great praise for his courage and bravery, but, fortunately for us, his army was not all composed of such brave men."

Soon after this second battle of Kellogg's Grove, Black Hawk moved up the Rock River across the border into Wisconsin around Lake Koshkonong, where the women and children had been hiding.

The day after the attack on Apple River Fort and the same day as the second battle of Kellogg's Grove, Americans won their first decisive victory in the war. On June 14, a small war party of Black Hawk's band attacked six men on the farm of Omri Spafford (near present-day Wiota, Wisconsin), killing four of them. In response, Henry Dodge led a company from Fort Dodge in search for the perpetrators. He spotted the Indians and gave chase, pinning them down in a bend of the Pecatonica River (Crawford County, Wisconsin). In just a few minutes, his company of twenty-nine men obliterated the war party of eleven (some say seventeen) with the loss of two men killed. One author said, "This was, all things considered, the most spirited and effective, fighting during the war." It definitely lifted American spirits. Up until this point, the Americans had primarily been on the defensive.

Chapter Eighteen

Wisconsin Heights

Beginning in late June, Atkinson's army, now numbering about 4000 men, started pursuing Black Hawk's band. Chief Shabonna and the half-breed Billy Caldwell, with about seventy-five Potawatomi, then soon joined the army. They were formed into a spy battalion to serve as scouts in front of the army. On June 30, the army crossed into Wisconsin near present-day Beloit. The army soon lost Black Hawk's trail, Reynolds stating that it was as if they "were hunting a shadow. "Meandering around the swamps and marshes of the Lake Koshkonong area, they soon ran low on food Atkinson dismissed many volunteers on July 10 (including Abraham Lincoln), temporarily suspended active offensive operations, and began building Fort Koshkonong. To save on supplies, Atkinson sent Posey and his volunteer brigade to Fort Hamilton to the west and most of the Potawatomi to Chicago. Meaningfully, for the forthcoming campaign he sent General Milton K. Alexander, General James Henry and Colonel Henry Dodge to Fort Winnebago (Portage, Wisconsin), about seventy miles from his camp, to obtain additional rations for the army.

Meanwhile, Black Hawk had traveled further up the Rock River with his starving band, now resorting to eating dead horses, digging up roots, and stripping bark from trees. His band started disintegrating as his approximately three hundred allied Winnebago, Potawatomi, and Kickapoo warriors now deserted. Food was scarce, and his band faced starvation.

Soon after arriving at Fort Winnebago, Pierre

Paquette, a local agent for the American Fur Company, informed Dodge that a Winnebago Indian in the area had notified him that Black Hawk's band was camped further up the Rock River forty miles to the east at Hustis Rapids (Hustisford, Wisconsin). Furthermore, Paquette offered that he and some Winnebagos would serve as guides. In the excitement of the opportunity to catch up with Black Hawk, General Henry, with his six hundred mounted Illinois volunteers, and Colonel Dodge, with his one hundred and fifty mounted volunteers, decided to disregard their orders to return to Atkinson and take up the pursuit of Black Hawk's band instead. Dodge believed that the Sauk would head further east and try to escape to Canada if not caught in time.

On the morning of July 15, General Alexander started his return trip to Atkinson, thirty miles away at Lake Koshkonong, with a pack train full of rations for the army. Led by seven or eight Winnebago guides General Henry and Colonel Dodge began their pursuit of Black Hawk; at the same time, they sent several messengers to ride to Atkinson to inform him of the news. Less than ten miles into their journey, they stumbled upon a fresh, extensive trail that they surmised belonged to Black Hawk's band. Abandoning their mission to Atkinson, the messengers returned to Henry and Dodge that night, surviving the poor aim of a sentry. The following morning, the army moved toward Black Hawk's trail. When the army reached Black Hawk's camp on July 19, they found it abandoned. Dodge and Henry wrote Atkinson that they had decided to continue their pursuit. Atkinson approved their decision, stating, "I have to urge and direct that you will press on with all haste and never lose sight of the object till the enemy is overtaken, defeated, and if possible captured."

Black Hawk's scouts had quickly detected the army's movement. In desperation and fear that the army would come and surround him, Black Hawk broke camp and headed for the Wisconsin River, planning to descend it on the north side to the Mississippi River, where he would cross and escape the Americans.

Dodge's and Henry's militiamen continued their dogged pursuit, reaching the Four Lakes region (Madison, Wisconsin) on July 20. They learned from a Winnebago man there that Black Hawk's Band was only a few miles ahead. The next day, they closely followed a trail littered with kettles, mats, and other goods. Their exhausting pursuit culminated in what became known as the Battle of Wisconsin Heights. Near present-day Sauk City, Wisconsin, Black Hawk's warriors fought a desperate rearguard action in the rain to hold off the Americans long enough to build enough watercraft to enable them to cross the river. Stevens' account of the final moments of pursuit and the battle is as follows:

> About noon the scouts fell upon two Indians and killed one while trying to escape. Dr. Addison Philleo at that moment scalped him, and for many years afterward was in the habit of exhibiting the scalp to strangers as a trophy of his valor in that war. The terrific pressure on the horses had been severely felt by this time, and before the day was half done forty or fifty of them gave out. About 3 o'clock the company of Capt. Joseph Dickson's spies reported the enemy reaching the bluffs of the Wisconsin River, which reanimated the troops with unusual vigor to increase their speed, and, if possible, overtake the enemy before he crossed the river. The men pushed on so rapidly that the rear guard of the Indians was overtaken, and, in order to occupy the whites, stopped frequently and engaged them with firing in order to allow the main body to cross the river. Twice Henry pressed them and twice the Indians gave way, but the third time Dickson's scouts or spies drove them to the main

body, which had reached a body of timber sufficiently dense to offer protection, and here the whole force of Indians made a stand.

Dismounting, every tenth man was detailed to hold horses, excepting the regiment of Colonel Fry, which was made the reserve and held to prevent the enemy from turning the flanks of the whites.

The Indians opened fire as the advance guard of the whites was passing a stretch of uneven ground, through the high grass and low brush. Major Ewing's Battalion was at once formed in front, where the Indians lured their fire into it from behind trees. In a few moments Henry arrived with the main army and formed the order of battle, Colonel Jones being placed to the right, Colonel Collins to the left, Fry in reserve and Ewing in front, with Dodge on the extreme right. In this order Henry ordered the forces to move. The order to charge the enemy was splendidly executed by Ewing, Jones and Collins, routing the Indians, who retreated to the right and concentrated before Dodge's Battalion, with the obvious intention of turning his flank. Henry sent Major McConnel to Dodge ordering him to charge the enemy, but this Dodge preferred to delay until he received a reinforcement, whereupon Henry sent Colonel Fry to his aid, and together they charged into the brush and high grass, receiving the fire of the whole body of the enemy.

Advancing and returning this fire, Dodge and Fry pursued the Indians with bayonets, driving them out with loss. Retreating rapidly, the enemy fell back to the west and took up a new and stronger position in the thick timber and tall grass at the head of a hollow leading to the Wisconsin River bottom. A determined stand was made here, but Ewing,

Jones and Collins dashed upon them and drove them in scattered squads down into the Wisconsin bottoms, covered with a swale so high that pursuit in the gathering darkness was impossible, and Herny, withdrawing his forces, lay all night on the field.

During the night a sonorous voice was heard from a neighboring hill, supposedly giving orders to the enemy, but as nothing came of it, no commotion or preparation to renew the fight followed. It proved to have been Ne-a-pope suing for peace in the tongue of the Winnebagoes, supposing that the guides and interpreter present from that nation would understand and secure a parley, but as all the Winnebagoes had fled in the beginning of the action, his words were wasted. Had he been understood, no doubt can exist but Henry would have closed the war then and there, for Black Hawk now realized that he was no longer fighting Stillman's command. The loss of the Indians was sixty-eight in killed and many more wounded, twenty-five of whom were found dead on the trail, subsequently resumed, while the loss to Henry was but one man Killed and eight wounded…

The following morning Henry advanced to the Wisconsin, only to find the enemy had retreated during the night across the river to the hills beyond. Had supplies been plenty, he would have pressed his victory by following, but being in great need of provisions, he was compelled to fail back to the base at Blue Mounds.

Black Hawk's account of the Battle from the Life of Black Hawk

Ne-a-pope, with a party of twenty, remained in our rear, to watch for the enemy, whilst we were proceeding to the Ouisconsin, with our women and children. We arrived, and had commenced crossing them to an island, when we discovered a large body of the enemy coming towards us. We were now compelled to fight, or sacrifice our wives and children to the fury of the whites! I met them with fifty warriors, (having left the balance to assist our women and children in crossing.) about a mile from the river, when an attack immediately commenced. I was mounted on a fine horse, and was pleased to see my warriors so brave. I addressed them in a loud voice, telling them to stand their ground, and never yield it to the enemy. At this time I was on the rise of a hill, where I wished to form my warriors, that we might have some advantage over the whites. But the enemy succeeded in gaining this point, which compelled us to fall back into a deep ravine, from which we continued firing at them and they at us, until it began to grow dark. My horse having been wounded twice during this engagement, and fearing from his loss of blood, that he would soon give out--and finding that the enemy would not come near enough to receive our fire, in the dusk of the evening-and knowing that our women and children had had sufficient time to reach the island in the Ouisconsin, I ordered my warriors to return, in different routes, and meet me at the Ouisconsin-and were astonished to find that the enemy were not disposed to pursue us.

In this skirmish, with fifty braves, I

defended and accomplished my passage over the Wisconsin, with a loss of only six men; though opposed by a host of mounted militia. I would not have fought there, but to gain time for my women and children to cross to an island. A warrior will duly appreciate the embarrassments I labored under- and whatever may be the sentiments of the *white people,* in relation to this battle, my nation, though fallen, will award to me the reputation of a great brave, in conducting it.

Years after the battle, Jefferson Davis praised Black Hawk's actions during the struggle: "A feat of most consummate management and bravery, in the face of an enemy of greasy superior numbers. I have never read of anything that could be compared with it. Had it been performed by white men, it would have been immortalized as one of the most splendid achievements in military history."

The flight of Black Hawk's band after the fight would set the stage for the last tragic battle of the war, a tragedy that could have been avoided as Neapope had been attempting to surrender the entire band, asking permission to cross the Mississippi.

Chapter Nineteen

Bad Axe

After the battle of Wisconsin Heights, Atkinson's army again pursued Black Hawk's band. The last troops had passed the river on the 28th and moved up the Wisconsin River three or four miles. The enemy's trail was discovered bearing downstream and followed by turning the columns to the left, then pursuing it twelve or fifteen miles over a flat and sandy prairie, which terminated at a deep creek, where the army camped for the night.

Stevens's description of the events leading up to the war's final battle is as follows.

> From this point, the trail was pursued with vigor all day over a rough, almost mountainous country, passing several of the enemy's encampments, which clearly indicated how hard he was pressed for provisions, horseflesh alone being left to him. The bodies of Indians who had died from the lack of proper dressing of their wounds were here seen in more significant numbers than before. Reaching the summit of a very high hill, the horses were tied up without food because of the lack of grass to eat amongst the timber.
>
> All day on the 30th, the march continued over a similar country. On the 31st, about fifteen miles were made over an unusually hilly country thickly timbered. At evening the first stream flowing west was reached and crossed, the army camping with six miles of the Kickapoo River. On

August 1st, the Kickapoo was crossed at ten o'clock at a shallow ford where commenced another rough prairie covered with growths of oak timber. It was a long day's march for the troops because they were forced to go further than usual for water. The trail indicated the immediate presence of the enemy and if darkness had not prevented them, the enemy could have been reached very soon. The camp was made that night near a small spring. Here Atkinson gave orders to be prepared at two o'clock the following morning to move for the bank of the Mississippi.

As Captain Throckmorton, commanding the Warrior, was ascending the river, he noticed a band of Indians near a camp on the bottoms at the mouth of the Bad Axe hoisting a white flag. Suspecting treachery, he ordered them to send a boat on board for a conference, which they declined. Without comment, except to allow fifteen minutes to remove their squaws and children, he shot a six-pounder into their midst, following it for an hour with a heavy fire of musketry, which cost the Indians many lives. Needing fuel to continue the contest, the boat fell down the river to Prairie du Chien to wood up preparatory to returning the following day and finishing the action, but by the hour of its return the battle of the Bad Axe had been finished and Black Hawk's race was run.

Promptly at 2 the morning of the 2d the troops rose, hastily ate breakfast and by sunrise resumed their march.

Black Hawk was aware of the presence of Atkinson's forces, and to give time for a retreat across the river deployed a party of about twenty to meet the enemy, commence the attack, and by gradual retreats turn him three or four miles above the camp.

About one hour after sunrise the rising fogs indicated the presence of the river and Dickson's spies were sent forward; they soon returned with a report that the enemy was drawn up in position and near at hand. Dodge thereupon ordered Dickson forward to reconnoiter the enemy and occupy his attention while he drew up his line and reported to Atkinson. This Dickson did, killing eight of the enemy. The regulars under Taylor and Alexander and Posey were ordered forward. The regulars immediately in Dodd's rear moved forward on his right; Dodge's men, dismounting, moved forward at the left in extended order for some minutes before Posey's command came up. This officer was posted on the right of the regulars and Alexander on his right, while Henry, trudging along with baggage, came upon the scene-just in time to be ordered to send Fry's regiment to Atkinson, which was done.

When forces moved against the Indian decoys, they of course gave way and were hotly followed by the whites.

Henry clearly saw the stratagem when Major Ewing discovered and reported to him the main trail leading to the river lower down. This trail he rapidly followed to the foot of the high bluff bordering on the bottoms, covered with timber, driftwood and underbrush, through which the trail ran. Halting here and leaving the horses, he formed his men on foot and advanced, after first sending forward a forlorn hope of eight men to draw the enemy's fire. These eight men boldly advanced until they were in sight of the river, when they were suddenly fired upon by a party of Indians and five of the eight men fell. Retreating to the cover of trees, the other three stood their ground until Henry came up.

Deploying his men to the right and left from the center, a charge was made and the battle began along the whole line. At this time Henry dispatched Major McConnel to Atkinson to report the presence of the entire force, which massed after the first charge and, with the loss of Fry's regiment, was now larger than Henry's force.

The Indians fought desperately from tree to tree, falling back step by step until the river was reached, when by a bayonet charge they were driven into the river. Some tried to swim; others took shelter in a small willow island nearby. This charge practically ended the battle, when Atkinson Dodge, Posey and Alexander, hearing the continued heavy firing, and receiving Major Mc Donnel's message, came up, and while Henry's men were finishing the fight, poured a galling fire into the vanishing, remnant, which killed many women and children, to the sincere regret of all, but as many of the squaws were dressed as men and mingled freely with them, it was a misfortune none could have foreseen or avoided.

To put the finishing strokes to Black Hawk's power, Dodge, Fry and Ewing, with the regulars under Taylor, Bliss, Harney and Smith, plunged breast deep into the water to the willow island, where most of the remaining Indians had taken a last stand and where in the face of a heavy fire the whites either killed, captured or drove them into the river. It was there in that little side contest that the greatest loss was supposed to have occurred to the whites, whose casualties in the engagement were twenty-four killed and wounded, while that of the enemy were upward of one hundred and fifty, forty captured, mostly women and children, and about forty or fifty horses taken. The loss to the regulars was five killed and four wounded; to Dodge six wounded; Posey one wounded; Alexander one wounded, and Henry seven killed and wounded.

The Sauk also lost an indeterminate number of lives when many of them had attempted to go down the Wisconsin River by canoes to cross the Mississippi. Dodge had warned Gustavus Loomis, the Commander of Fort Crawford, of the Sauk movement and advised him to stop the attempt. Loomis then sent twenty-five troops to the mouth of the Wisconsin on a flatboat with a six-pound cannon. Sometime on the night of July 29, the soldiers fired on the canoes, trying to slide past them. In addition, Colonels Blackburn and Archer crossed the river with one hundred and fifty men and fruitlessly searched the islands and bottoms, but did not find any survivors.

As the trail of the fleeing fugitives indicated that they had gone along the Iowa River, a party of Sioux called upon General Atkinson to receive permission to follow the approximately two hundred fugitives who had made it across the river. The Sioux attacked the survivors, taking an additional sixty-eight scalps and capturing Neapope. Thus, the war was ended in which perhaps as many as 450-1000 Indians perished along with seventy-two hundred soldiers and civilians. The attitude of many of the people during this period was summed up by participant John Wakefield, who stated after the massacre at Bad Axe: "I must confess that it filled by heart with gratitude and joy, to think that I had 'been instrumental, with many others, in delivering my country from those merciless savages, and restoring those people (of the frontier region) again to their peaceful homes and firesides."

Black Hawk's Escape and Capture

Meanwhile, Black Hawk, his sons, and the Prophet escaped immediate capture. Seeing the lost battle, Black Hawk fled north, hoping to find a temporary refuge among his former friends, the Winnebago of the Lemonweir valley. The Sauk disapproved of Black Hawk's desertion as they felt that he had brought ruin to them and had run off to save his own life.

Black Hawk found a secure hiding place and hid there for two entire days and nights. Toward the evening of the third day, he saw two Winnebago chiefs, Chaetar and One-Eyed Decora, both former friends, approach his hiding place and set up camp for the night. Before they slept, Black Hawk overheard them discussing their plans to make him their prisoner. During the night, Black Hawk fled with the Prophet to Prairie La Crosse, one hundred miles further up the Mississippi, and then crossed to the west side. The next day, Chaetar and Decora picked up his trail. After a few more days, they sighted Black Hawk at a camp on Little Lake, near present-day Tomah, Wisconsin. They entered a wigwam and proceeded to capture him alive. (Another account states that a different Winnebago discovered Black Hawk's hiding place and reported it to his chief. The Winnebago chief summoned Black Hawk to his village, where he was persuaded to give himself up. Black Hawk then left with the Winnebago chief, Wabokieshiek to surrender himself to Joseph General Street at Prairie du Chien on August 27.

When he surrendered, Black Hawk is reported saying to the General:

"My warriors fell around me. It began to look dismal. I saw my evil day at hand. The sun rose clear on us in the morning; at night it sunk in a dark cloud and looked like a ball of fire. This was the last sun that shone on Black Hawk. He is now a prisoner to the White man, but he can stand the torture. He is not afraid of death. He is no coward. Black Hawk is an Indian. He has done nothing of which an Indian need be ashamed. He has fought the battles of his country against the white man, who came year after year to cheat his people and take away their lands. You know the cause of our making war. It is known to all white men. They ought to be ashamed of it. The white men despise the Indians and drive them from their homes. but the Indians are not deceitful. Indians do not steal. Black Hawk is satisfied. He will go to the world of spirits contented. he has done his duty. His father will meet and reward him. The white man do not scalp the heads, but they do worse--they poison the heart. It is not pure with them. His countrymen will not be scalped, but they will in a few years become like the white man, so that you cannot hurt them; and there must be, as in the white settlements, as many officers as men to take care of them and keep them in order. Farewell to my nation! Farewell to Black Hawk!"

Lieutenant Jefferson Davis brought Black Hawk down the Mississippi to Jefferson Barracks in St. Louis, where he was imprisoned In April 1833, Black Hawk was taken to Washington D.C. After meeting with President Andrew Jackson, he was imprisoned in Fortress Monroe for six weeks. Upon release, he visited Baltimore, Philadelphia, New York, Buffalo, and Detroit before returning to Fort Armstrong around August 1st. Black Hawk was astounded by the population and strength of the United States and promised never to fight against the Americans in the future. In 1837, he returned to

Washington, D.C. as part of a delegation. Black Hawk lived in peace for the next five years near Keokuk's village in a lodge of peeled bark with his wife, two sons, and a daughter. Black Hawk then moved to a new home by the Des Moines River near Iowaville, Iowa, where he died in 1838 at the age of seventy-two.

Aftermath

Before signing a peace treaty, Scott had carried instructions from the Secretary of War. The terms he was to impose on the defeated tribes required all a tribe's lands east of the Mississippi if most of its members had fought against the United States. For a tribe with less than a majority fighting against the Americans, he was to take a proportion of the land equal to the proportion of the tribe engaged in hostilities. Governor of Illinois, John Reynolds, served with him as co-commissioner.

Scott concluded a treaty on September 21, 1832, with the Sauk and Fox after Black Hawk had departed for St. Louis. In the treaty, he obtained a cession of land fifty miles wide west of the Mississippi, extending almost the entire length of the state of Iowa. For $660,000, $20,000 in specie was to be paid each year for thirty years to the United States (the land was estimated to be worth $7,000,000). To ensure there would be no future uncertainties concerning the treaty terms, the Indians had to vacate the land by June 1, 1833, and never again be allowed to "reside, plant, fish, or hunt on any portion of the ceded land. The United States would also provide an additional black and gunsmith shop for the tribes for thirty years, along with annual tobacco deliveries, and salt would be made. Immediately, the government would provide food (beef cattle, pork, flour, and salt to sustain the tribes through the coming winter and 6,000 bushels of corn to be delivered the following April.

The Black Hawk War had lasted a mere four months and cost about three million dollars. About two hundred whites lost their lives, and probably less than three hundred of Black Hawk's band remained alive. Fought only one hundred and sixty years after the French began establishing a presence in Illinois, the Black Hawk War ended the Indian occupation of Illinois. The Potawatomi, who had aided the Americans in the war and were also forced to leave Illinois, were the last tribe to be removed following the Treaty in Chicago in 1833. As a result, today, there are no federally recognized Indian tribes living in Illinois.

Summary Part IV Black Hawk War

Black Hawk fought an avoidable war, losing against incredible odds. Though Black Hawk and the Sauk gained sympathy due to the slaughter at Bad Axe, it did not earn them any substantive compensation. The British Band was still removed from Illinois and integrated with most of the tribe on their Iowa land. The war served to increase the strong American desire to remove the remaining Indians living in Illinois.

In 1836, the Sauk and Fox sold a small portion of their land and, in 1837, sold about 1.25 million acres) of their land. They surrendered their remaining land in Iowa a little over five years later. They moved Kansa south of the Missouri River, sharing a 435,200-acre reservation with Ottawa, Chippewas, and Kansas Indians. After another treaty in 1867, they relocated to their final destination, the Indian Territory, in Oklahoma.

Although settlement growth in Illinois slowed during the war, the pace picked up soon. In 1830, the population had been 157,445, according to the Federal census. By the State census in 1835, the population had exploded to 272,427. Also, in 1831, eight federal land offices sold a total of one-third of a million acres of land. In 1836, ten land offices sold three million acres. By 1840, Illinois ranked fourteen out of twenty-six states in population with 476,000 inhabitants. In the late 1830s, railroads were beginning to be built, and the national road would reach Illinois in 1840. Illinois was well on its way to becoming one of the great states in the federal union.

Conclusion

The beautiful and bountiful land of Illinois has been won in battle by the white man. Most known historical battles were fought in this sparsely settled state by armies and groups of a few hundred men or less. The state has remained at peace since the last battle was fought in Illinois against a foreign foe almost two hundred years ago. Yet, no one knows the future, as wars have plagued humanity throughout history. Hopefully, millions of Illinoisans can remain at peace and keep the land their ancestors won by shedding their blood.

Appendix 1

1804 Treaty

Articles of a Treaty, made at St. Louis, in the district of Louisiana, between William Henry Harrison, Governor of the Indians Territory and the District of Louisiana, Superintendent of Indian affairs for the said Territory and district and Commissioner plenipotentiary of the United States, for concluding any treaty or treaties, which may be found necessary with any of the Northwestern tribes of Indians, of the one part; and the Chiefs and head men of the united Sac and Fox tribes of the other part.

Article 1. The United States receive the united Sac and Fox tribes into their friendship and protection and the said tribes agree to consider themselves under the protection of the United States, and no other power whatsoever.

Art. 2 The General boundary line between the land of the United States and the said Indian tribes shall be as follows, to wit: Beginning at a point on the Missouri River opposite to the mouth of the Gasconade River; thence, in a direct course so as to strike the River Jeffreon, at the distance of 30 miles from its mouth and down the said Jeffreon to the Mississippi; thence, up the Mississippi to the mouth of the Ouisconsing River, and up the same to a point which shall be 36 miles in a direct line from the mouth of the said river, thence, by a direct line to the point where the Fox River (a branch of the Illinois) leaves the small Lake called Sakaegan; thence, down the Fox River to the Illinois River, and down the same to the Mississippi. And the said tribes, for and in consideration of the friendship and protection of the United States, which is now extended to them, of the goods (to the value of two thousand two hundred and thirty-four dollars and fifty cents) which are now delivered, and of the annuity hereinafter stipulated to be paid, do herby cede and relinquish forever, to the United States, all the lands included within the above described boundary.

Art. 3. In consideration of the cession and relinquishment of land made in the preceding article, the United States will deliver to the said tribes, at the town of St. Louis, or some other convenient place on the Mississippi, yearly and every year, goods suited to the circumstances of the Indians of the value of one thousand dollars (six hundred of which are intended for the Sacs and four hundred for the Fox), reckoning that value at the first cost of the goods in the City or place in the United States, where they shall be procured. And if the said tribes shall hereafter at an annual delivery of the goods aforesaid, desire that a part of their annuity should be furnished in domestic animals implements of husbandry, and other utensils, convenient for them, or in compensation to useful artificers, who may reside with or near them, and be employed for their benefit, the same shall, at the subsequent annual delivery, be furnished accordingly.

Art. 4 The United States will never interrupt the said tribes in the possession of the lands, which they rightfully claim, but will, on the contrary, protect them in the quiet enjoyment of the same against their own citizens and against all other white persons, who may intrude upon them. And the said tribes do hereby engage that they will never sell their lands, or any party thereof, to any sovereign power but the United States, nor to the citizens or subjects of any other sovereign power, nor to the citizens of the United States.

Art. 5 Lest the friendship, which is now established between the United States and the said Indian Tribes should be interrupted by the misconduct of individuals, it is hereby agreed that for injuries done by individuals no private revenge or retaliation shall take place, but instead thereof, complaint shall be made by the party injured to the other by the said tribe, or either of them, to the superintendent of Indian affairs, or one of his deputies; and by the superintendent, or other person appointed by the President, to the Chiefs of the said tribes. And it shall be the duty of the said chiefs, upon complaint being made, as aforesaid, to deliver up the person, or persons, against who the complaint is made, to the end that he or they may be punished agreeably to the laws of the state or territory where the offense may have been committed. And, in like manner, if any robbery, violence or murder shall be committed on any Indian, or Indians, belonging to the said tribes, or either of them, the person or persons so offending shall be tried, and, if found guilty, punished in the like manner as if the injury had been done to a white man. And, it is farther agreed, that the chiefs of the said tribes shall, to the utmost of their power, exert themselves to recover horses or other property which may be stolen from any citizen or citizens of the United States by any individual or individuals of their tribes. And the property so recovered shall be forthwith delivered to the superintendent or other person authorized to receive it that it may be restored to the proper owner. And in cases where the exertions of the chiefs shall be ineffectual in recovering the property stolen, as aforesaid, if sufficient proof can be obtained, that such property was actually stolen by any Indian or Indians belonging to the said tribes, or either of them, the United States may deduct from the annuity of the said tribes, a sum equal to the value of the property which has been stolen, And the United States hereby guarantee to any Indian or Indians of the said tribes a full indemnification for any horses, or other property so stolen from them, by any of their citizens; Provided, that the property so stolen cannot be recovered, and that sufficient proof is produced that it was actually stolen by a citizen of the United States.

Art. 6. If any citizen of the United States, or any other white person, should form a settlement, upon the lands which are the property of the Sac and Fox tribes, upon complaint being made thereof, to the superintendent, or other person having charge of the affairs of the Indians, such intruders shall forthwith be removed.

Art 7. As long as the lands which are now ceded to the United States remain their property, the Indians belonging to the said tribes shall enjoy the privilege of living and hunting upon them.

Art. 8. As the laws of the United States regulating trade and intercourse with the Indian tribes are already extended to the country inhabited by the Sauks and Fox, and as it is provided by those laws, that no person shall reside as a trader, in the Indian country, without a license, under the hand and seal of the Superintendent of Indian Affairs, or other person appointed for the purpose by the President, the said tribes do promise and agree that they will not suffer any trader to reside amongst them without such license, and that they will, from time to time, give notice to the Superintendent, or to the Agent, for their tribes, of all the traders that may be in their country.

Art. 9. In order to put a stop to the abuses and impositions, which are practiced upon the said tribes by the private traders, the United States, will, at a convenient time, establish a trading house, or factory, where the individuals of the said tribes can be supplied with goods at a more reasonable rate than they have been accustomed to procure them.

Art. 10. In order to evince the sincerity of their friendship and affection for the United States, and a respectful reference for their advice, by an act which will not only be acceptable to them, but by the Common Father of all the nations of the Earth, the said tribes do, hereby solemnly promise and agree that they will put an end to the bloody war which has heretofore raged between their tribes and those of the great and little Osages. And for the purpose of burying the tomahawk and renewing the friendly intercourse between themselves and the Osages, a meeting of their respective Chiefs shall take place, at which, under the direction of the above named Commissioner, or the Agent of Indian affairs residing at St. Louis, an adjustment of all their differences shall be made and peace established, upon a firm and lasting basis.

Art. 11. As it is probable that the Government of the United States will establish a Military Post at, or near the mouth, of the Oisconsing River, and as the land on the lower side of the River may not be suitable for that purpose, the said tribes hereby agree, that a Fort may be built, either on the upper side of the Oisconsing, or on the right bank of the Mississippi, as the one or the other may be found most convenient; and a tract of land not exceeding two miles square, shall be given for that purpose. And the said tribes do further agree, that they will at all times, allow to traders and other persons traveling through their country, under the authority of the United States, a free and safe passage for themselves and their property of every description. And that for such passage, they shall at no time, and no account whatever, be subject to any toll or exaction.

Art. 12. This Treaty shall take effect and be obligatory on the contracting parties, as soon as the same shall have been ratified by the President, by and with the advice and consent of the Senate of the United States.

In testimony whereof, the said William Henry Harrison, and the Chiefs and headmen of the said Sac and Fox tribes, have hereunto set their hands and affixed their seals. Done at Saint Louis, in the district of Louisiana, on the third day of November, One Thousand Eight Hundred and Four, and of the independence of the United States the Twenty-Ninth.

Appendix II

Abraham Lincoln and Other Famous People Who Served in the Black Hawk War

Abraham Lincoln

In April 1832, Abraham Lincoln learned of Governor John Reynold's call for four hundred volunteers from Sangamon County for thirty days. Lincoln quit his job at a failing store and signed up. Already known for his strength, prowess as a wrestler, and storytelling abilities, three-quarters of the men in his company elected the twenty-three-year-old Lincoln as their captain. On April 28, Lincoln was mustered into service and marched to the Rock River, arriving on May 7. General Henry Atkinson soon mustered him into the U.S. service. Lincoln suffered humiliation and was reprimanded twice, once for firing a gun against orders and again when his men were found intoxicated. As punishment, Lincoln was confined for a day and had to wear a wooden sword. After the second incident, his men became a model company. In one incident, while on the march, one of Lincoln's men wanted to kill an old Potawatomi man they came upon, but Lincoln prevented him. On May 27, Lincoln was mustered out of the service.

Lincoln reenlisted as a private in Elijah Iles' company for twenty days of service. During their time in Galena, one member of Iles' company later confessed that he and several others visited the whorehouses there but, did not say if Lincoln was one of them. After Lincoln was mustered out, he enlisted in Captain Jacob M. Early's company on June 16 for a third term of service. During his service, Lincoln spent time scouring the country in search of Indians and traveled as far as Lake Koshkonong in Wisconsin. Three times, he arrived at a battlefield the day after a battle, after Stillman's run, Kellogg's Grove, and Apple River Fort. Lincoln was mustered out of service on July 10. He eventually received from the federal government a land bounty of forty acres in Iowa and one hundred and twenty acres in Illinois.

Years after the war, when criticizing General Lewis Cass's effort to brag about his service in the Black Hawk War, Lincoln said: "If General Cass went in advance of me in picking whortleberries, I guess I surpassed him in charges upon the wild onions. If he saw any live fighting Indians, it was more than I did, but I had a good many bloody experiences with the mosquitoes; and although I never fainted from loss of blood, I can truly say I was often very hungry."

Lincoln's friend and biographer stated that Lincoln mentioned the presence of future Confederate President Jefferson Davis in the Black Hawk War. Lincoln may have met Jefferson Davis on occasion and even been served a meal with him at John Dixon's post by his ferry on the Rock River during his service. Author Frank E. Stevens stated that Davis stayed at Dixon's post from late May until June 27, when Lincoln also visited the post during his assignments.

Zachary Taylor

Zachary Taylor served as a Colonel of the First Infantry Regiment under General Henry Atkinson during the Black Hawk War. He also fought in the 2nd Seminole War, winning a battle at Lake Okeechobee in 1837. Later in the War with Mexico, Taylor's victories in the battles of Palo Alto, Resaca de la Palma, Monterrey, and Buena

Vista, where he pitted his 4600 men against Santa Anna's army of 15,000 troops helped propel him to the Whig nomination for the presidency in 1848. In the contest against Democrat Lewis Cass, he became the only person besides Lincoln to attain the nation's highest elected office. Taylor died in 1850 in the middle of his term.

Winfield Scott

Winfield Scott, already a General at the beginning of the Black Hawk War, would never be directly involved in any action. President Andrew Jackson had sent Scott on a mission to end the war when he left Fortress Monroe on the East Coast with nine companies under his command. Unfortunately, even before Scott made it to Chicago, a cholera epidemic decimated his troops. By the time Scott left Fort Dearborn in Chicago, only two hundred out of the eight hundred and fifty men who had left Buffalo, New York, were fit for field operations. When Scott reached Prairie du Chien, the war was over. After the Black Hawk War, Scott commanded in the 2nd Seminole War, oversaw the Cherokee Removal, and was promoted to Major General in command of the U.S. Anny in 1841. His greatly admired Veracruz campaign and the winning of the battles of Cerro Gordo, Contreras, Churubusco, Molino del Rey, and Chapultepec on his way to capturing Mexico City vaulted him into the race for the Whig Presidential nomination in 1848, which Taylor won. Scott would win the Whig Presidential nomination in 1852 only to lose against Franklin Pierce in the general election. Scott became the only Lieutenant General in the U.S. Army after George Washington in 1855. He was forced into retirement in 1861, also dying that year.

Jefferson Davis

Jefferson Davis was Lieutenant Zachary Taylor's adjutant during the Black Hawk War. He later fought with distinction under Zachary Taylor at the battles of Monterrey and Buena Vista during the War with Mexico. At Buena Vista, where he was wounded, Davis valiantly led Mississippi riflemen in repulsing a charge by Mexican lancers, helping to win the victory. Davis later was a senator from Mississippi from 1847-1851 and 1857-1861 and served as Secretary of War under Franklin Pearce from 1853-1857. He was a Major General in charge of Mississippi's defense before he was notified by telegram that he had been chosen as the provisional President of the Confederate States of America. Though Davis would have preferred to lead men in battle, he accepted and led the Confederacy through the Civil War. He died in 1889.

Henry Dodge

Henry Dodge would later serve as Territorial Governor of Wisconsin from 1836-141 and 1845-1848. He would also serve as a U.S. senator.

A few of the other prominent men (not all) who served in the war and later achieved a measure of military fame were Lieutenant Albert Sydney Johnston, acclaimed to be the most competent Jr. officer in the Black Hawk War) (Civil War General), Lieutenant Robert Anderson, (who mustered Lincoln into the service the second time and commanded at Fort Sumter in1861, and later a Brigadier General), Captain W.S. Harney (Civil War General), Private John A. Mc Clernand (Civil War General), and Joseph E. Johnston (Civil War General).

Appendix III

Reconstructed Forts in Illinois Today

Fort Massac

The British planned to garrison Fort Massac in 1764 after the French and Indian War but were delayed due to Pontiac's Rebellion. When Captain Stirling arrived in 1765, he only found the burned ruins that the Chickasaw Indians had left. The site of Fort Massac remained unoccupied until 1794. Under orders from President George Washington, who feared threats from the Spanish just west of the Mississippi, General Anthony Wayne sent a detail to build a new fort there. Major Thomas Doyle and Captain Issac Guion's company of the First Sub legion, plus a detachment of artillery, built a new fort beginning in May and completing it in October. The best description of the fort comes from Victor Collot, who visited in 1796 and stated that the fort had four blockhouses surrounded by a ditch and was about seventy feet above the river at low water. The structure was believed to be approximately forty- six yards square on each side, with palisades of upright logs twenty feet high.

The fort and its site would prove useful for several future important occasions and events. For example, upriver from Fort Massac in Hardin County, Illinois, thieves, river pirates, murderers, and counterfeiters operated out of Cave-in-Rock. Cave-in-Rock is a cave along the Ohio River about fifty-five feet wide at its base with a semi- elliptical opening that extends back from the opening, about one hundred sixty feet with an average width of forty feet. It was a natural hideout for criminals preying on travels down the Ohio River. In the late 1790s, a counterfeiter named Duff made it his base. Eventually he met his demise due to the action taken by the commander at Fort Massac.

According to the most repeated version, six soldiers apprehended Duff, his slave Pompey, and three members of his gang upriver from Cave-in-Rock. They put them in a boat and, while descending the river on their return to the fort, stopped at Cave-in-Rock to have dinner. One of them stood guard on the boat. Having only four sets of manacles, they left Pompey free, believing he would not care about his master. Instead, Pompey helped free one of the prisoners, and together, they overpowered the guard and freed the other two men. They grabbed the guns stacked near the boat, rushed to the cave, and captured their captors. The gang then secured all the soldiers into the boat and sent it floating down the river.

The soldiers were sighted while passing Fort Massac and were ordered to stop, which, of course, they could not. The commander discovered what happened when a skiff he had sent to apprehend them returned. Angered by the outcome, he determined to get his revenge by bringing a Canadian and three Indians to kill Duff. He promised them a reward for a successful mission. They caught and killed Duff and his slave, while the rest of the gang fled. Also, in 1799, the U.S. Treasury operated a customs office from the fort. The office required all commercial boats to stop and pay truces on their cargo.

Tensions flared again in 1802 between America and Spain when Spanish authorities stopped American trade down the Mississippi by revoking American rights to deport their cargoes in New Orleans. Wooden forts lasted only briefly, and Fort Massac was no exception. By 1802, the fort had already deteriorated. Hence, it was decided that the fort would be rebuilt once again. Captain Daniel Bissel's First Infantry Regiment rebuilt it in 1802. By 1803, Bissel and other river post commanders were ordered to oppose any unauthorized American forces rumored to be gathering for an attack on Louisiana.

Additional highlights in the fort's history were as follows: The Lewis and Clark expedition stopped at the fort late the following year and recruited several garrison members for their Corps of Discovery, including George Drouillard. Drouillard played a vital role as an interpreter and hunter on the expedition. In the War of 1812, the government utilized Fort Massac as a training center for Western recruits sent east to fight the British. The Fort was evacuated in 1814. By 1817, the fort had been dismantled by local inhabitants, who had used the wood for their own buildings. Wood was also taken as fuel for steamboats on the Ohio River. The site's final use came with the Civil War's start. Camp Massac was established to thwart any Confederate forces that may use the Ohio River. However, it was soon abandoned after a measles outbreak killed a substantial number of troops in 1861-1862.

In the early 1970s, a replica of the 1794 American fort was reconstructed near Metropolis, Illinois, about a mile west of the original site. It was dismantled in the fall of 2002. Illinois then built a historically accurate replica of the 1802 American fort in 2003, standing east of the original French and American forts.

The current fort consists of a stockade wall, three blockhouses, and a picketed dry moat with an officer's quarters and two barracks. The officers' quarters are a sixteen by twenty-two-foot two-story building built on a stone foundation constructed of white oak timber with a brick fireplace on each floor. There are two barracks for soldiers; the east one is eighteen by seventy-five feet with a porch, and the west is twenty-two by seventy-five feet. Both consist of two stories with four rooms, each with a fireplace inside. A sixteen-by-sixteen-foot two-story blockhouse is on the northwest corner. A twenty-by-twenty-four-foot two-story blockhouse is on the southwest corner, the same as the 1794-style fort. The southeast blockhouse is sixteen by sixteen feet and has three floors. The third floor is a lookout tower over the Ohio River.

Fort Chartres

After George Rogers Clark captured Kaskaskia and Cahokia, he never proceeded to Fort de Chartres since the British had evacuated it in 1771-1772. As settlers moved into the area around the abandoned fort in the 1790s, they dismantled the remains to procure stone for their own use. In 1812, Governor Ninian Edwards took five cannons from the Fort's ruins and mounted them at Fort Russell.

Eventually, the State of Illinois purchased the site in 1913. At that time, the powder magazine was all that remained of the original structure. Workers began restoring the powder magazine in 1917. In the 1920s, they exposed portions of other buildings and wall foundations. In the 1930s, the Works Progress Administration reconstructed the gateway and two stone buildings.

Today, visitors can see a partially reconstructed north wall with bastions, a gatehouse, musket ports, and embrasures. Other structures include the guards' house and the King's storehouse, which house the Piethman Museum containing items discovered in archaeological research of the area. The Fort is four miles west of Prairie du Rocher, Illinois, on state Route 155.

Apple River Fort

After the Black Hawk War, two squatter families named Hawk and Davis occupied the fort. The hastily built fort lasted until 1847 when George Bainbridge purchased the land from the federal government. He dismantled the fort and used the lumber to construct a barn.

The fort is in Elizabeth, Illinois, named in honor of

the heroism displayed by Elizabeth Armstrong during Black Hawk's attack on the fort. The Illinois State Historical Society in Jo Davies County erected a replica fort in 1934. In 1995, the Apple River Fort Historic Foundation determined to locate the original fort site. Archaeologists excavated the site and recovered numerous artifacts. In 1996, volunteers rebuilt the fort's two cabins, erected a surrounding palisade of fourteen-to-fifteen-foot logs placed in a two to three-foot trench, constructed firing stands on two comers accessed by hand-hewn ladders, and added a two-story blockhouse with the upper story projecting two feet over the lower story.

Bibliography

Alvord, Clarence Walworth. *The Illinois Country 1673-1818.* Springfield, IL. Illinois Centennial Commission, 1920.

Bakeless, John. *Background to Glory.* Philadelphia J.B. Lippincott Company, 1957.

Brown, Margaret K, and Dean C. Lawrie. *The French Colony in the Mid-Mississippi Valley.* Carbondale, IL: American Kestrel Books, 1995.

Caldwell, Norman F. *Fort Massac: The American Frontier Post 1718-1805"* Journal of the Illinois State Historical Society n.s. 43 (summer 1950): 265 281.

Clark, George Rogers. *The Conquest of the Illinois.* Ed. By Milo Quaife, 1920; reprint, Bensenville; Arcadia press, 2 017.

Davis, James E. *Frontier Illinois.* Bloomington, IN: Indiana University Press, 1998. Edmunds, David R *The Potawatomi.* Norman, OK: University of Oklahoma Press, 1978.

Edmunds, Davi R. and Peyser, Joseph L. *The Fox Wars: The Mesquakie Challenge to New France.* Norman, OK: University of Oklahoma Press, 1963.

Edwards, Ninian W. *History of Illinois 1778-1833 and the Life and Times of Ninian Edwards,* Springfield, IL., Illinois State Journal Company. 1870.

Ferguson, Gillium. *Illinois in the War of 1812.* Urbana, IL: University of Illinois Press. 2012.

Gibson, A.M. *The Kickapoos: Lords of the Middle Border.* Norman, OK: University of Oklahoma Press, 1993.

Gilpin, Alec R. *The War of 1812 in the Old Northwest.* East Lansing, OH: Michigan State University Press, 1958.

Hagan, William T. *The Sac and Fox Indians.* Norman, OK: University of Oklahoma Press, 1958.

Hall, Jonathan N. *Reconstructed Forts of the Old Northwest Territory.* Westminster, Maryland: Heritage Books, Inc., 2008.

Heckewelder, John. *History, Manners, and Customs of the Indian Nations: Who Once Inhabited Pennsylvania and the Neighboring States.* New and rev. ed. Philadelphia, 1876. Reprint ed. New York: Arno Press & the New York Times. 1971

Hickey, Donald R. *The War of 1812. A Forgotten Conflict.* Urbana, IL: University of Illinois Press, 1989.

History of Crawford & Richland Counties, Wisconsin, Springfield: Union Publishing Company. 1884.

Hitsman, Mackay J. *The Incredible War of 1812: A Military History,* Toronto: University of Toronto Press, 1965.

Jackson, Donald ed. *Ma-Ka-Tai-Me-She-Kia-Kiak, Black Hawk: An Autobiography.* 1955. Urbana, IL: University of Illinois Press, 1990.

Jung, Patrick J. *The Black Hawk War of 1812.* Norman, OK: University of Oklahoma Press, 2007.

Kling, Stephen A. *Battle for St. Louis: The Attack on Cahokia, and the American Revolution in the West.* St. Louis: THGC Publishing, 2017.

Mahon, John K. *The War of 1812.* Gainesville: University Presses of Florida, 1972.

Matson, Nehemiah. *The French and Indians of Illinois River.* 1874. Carbondale and Edwardsville, IL: Southern Illinois University Press, 2001.

Meese, William A. *The Battle of Campbell's Island,* Moline: 1904; reprint, London: Forgotten Books, 2012. Mink, Claudia G. *Cahokia: City of the Sun,* Collinsville: Cahokia Mounds Museum Society, 1992.

Osman, Eaton G. *Starved Rock: A Chapter of Colonial History.* Chicago: A. Flanagan Company, 1911.

Patterson, J.B. ed. *Ma-Ka-Toi-Me-She-Kia-Kiak, or Black Hawk.* 1834; reprint, Fairfield: Ye Galleon Press, 1998.

Peckham, Howard H. *Pontiac, and the Indian Uprising.* Princeton: Princeton University Press, 1947.

Pease, Theodore Colvin, *The Story of Illinois,* Chicago, London, University of Chicago Press, revised 3rd Edition 1965 by Marguerite Jenison Pease.

Quaife, Milo M. *Chicago and the Old Northwest 1673-1835.* 1913. University of Chicago Press, Urbana, 2001.

Stark, William F. *Along the Black Hawk Trail.* Sheboygan, WI: Zimmerman Press, 1984.

Stevens, Frank E. *The Black Hawk War, Including a Review of Black Hawk's Life.* Chicago: Frank E. Stevens, 1903.

___*Illinois in the War of 1812-1814,* "Transactions of the Illinois State Historical Society for 1904, 62-197.

Steward, John F. "Destruction of the Fox Indians in 1730." *Transactions of the Illinois State Historical Society for the Year 1902,* 184-54. Springfield: State Historical Society, 1903.

Sutton, Robert P., ed. *The Prairie State: A Documentary History of Illinois Colonial Years to 1860.* W. M. Eardmans Pub. Grand Rapids, MI, 1976.

Tanner, Helen Hornbeck. *Atlas of Great Lakes Indian History.* Norman, OK: University of Oklahoma Press, 1987. Temple, Wayne C. *Indian Villages of the Illinois Country.* Springfield, IL.: Illinois State Museum Scientific Papers 2(2), 1966.

Transactions of the United States Historical Society No. 9, Springfield: Phillips Bros. State Printers, 1904. Wakefield, John A. *Wakefield's History of the Black Hawk War,* 1834 Reprint of first Ed. by John Wakefield, by Frank Everett Stevens, Madison WI. Roger Hunt, 1976.

Wallace, Anthony F.C. *Prelude to Disaster.* Springfield, IL: Illinois State Historical Library, 1970.

Walczynski, Mark. *Massacre 1769: The Search For The Origin of The Legend of Starved Rock.* St. Louis Mo: The Center for French Colonial Studies, Inc., 2013.